2-18-75

CONVERSATIONS WITH KLEMPERER

CONVERSATIONS WITH KLEMPERER

compiled and edited by

PETER HEYWORTH

LONDON
VICTOR GOLLANCZ LTD
1973

© Otto Klemperer and Peter Heyworth 1973
First published May 1973
Second impression August 1973

ISBN 0 575 01652 3

ACKNOWLEDGEMENTS

The following illustrations are the copyright of Lotte Klemperer: all photographs on plates facing pp. 32, 33, 49 and 93; *c* facing page 65, *b* facing page 85, *c*, *d*, and *e* facing page 92. The woodcut by Ewald Dülberg facing page 48 is the copyright of Peter Dülberg.

The discography has been based on one made by F. F. Clough and G. J. Cuming, and used in *Minor Recollections* by Otto Klemperer (Dennis Dobson, 1964) by arrangement with *Audio and Record Review* (now *Hi-Fi News and Record Review*). It has been brought up to date by Malcolm Walker to include all discs made and issued as of 1 January 1973. It does not include commercial tapes.

Printed in Great Britain by
The Camelot Press Ltd, London and Southampton

Chronology

1885   Born in Breslau

1889   Family moved to Hamburg

1901   Hoch Conservatory, Frankfurt-am-Main

1902   Klindworth-Scharwenka Conservatory, Berlin

1906   Début as conductor in Offenbach's *Orpheus in the Underworld*, produced by Max Reinhardt

1907–1910   Assistant conductor, German Opera House, Prague

1910–1912   Assistant conductor, Hamburg Opera

1913–1914   Assistant conductor, Barmen Opera

1914–1917   Deputy musical director, Strasbourg Opera

1917–1924   Musical director, Cologne Opera

1924–1927   Musical director, Wiesbaden Opera

1924   Début in Moscow and Leningrad

1926   Début in New York

1927–1933   Berlin State Opera
(1927–1931 director and subsequently musical director of the Staatsoper am Platz der Republik—commonly known as the Kroll Opera. 1931–1933 at the Staatsoper unter den Linden)

1929   Début in London

1933–1939   Principal conductor, Los Angeles Philharmonic Orchestra

1947–1950   Budapest Opera

1951   First concert with the Philharmonia Orchestra, London

1959   Principal conductor for life of the Philharmonia Orchestra, London

1964   President and principal conductor for life of the New Philharmonia Orchestra

1972   Retirement

Contents

List of Illustrations

INTRODUCTION

by Peter Heyworth

IN THE SUMMER of 1969 Mr Robert Chesterman, of the Canadian Broadcasting Corporation, who had already recorded talks with other eminent conductors, asked me whether Otto Klemperer would agree to doing something similar. I was not optimistic. I knew of Dr Klemperer's distaste for interviews and the like, but I wrote explaining Mr Chesterman's project. To my surprise and delight I received an answer virtually by return of post. Dr Klemperer would not be interested in giving an interview in the usual meaning of the word, but if I could spare a few days he would like to talk more extensively about his life, his views on music and other matters. Accordingly, at the end of August Mr Chesterman and I arrived in Zürich, where Dr Klemperer lives. Such was the origin of these conversations.

Meanwhile the Westdeutsche Rundfunk of Cologne had got wind of what was afoot and, mindful of Dr Klemperer's approaching eighty-fifth birthday, asked me to raise the question of some sort of interview in German, however brief. I was naturally loath to do so, as I felt I had already trespassed far enough on Dr Klemperer's good will. On the last day of the Canadian conversations I did, however, mention the matter to his daughter and that afternoon she told me that her father would be willing to do a similar series of conversations in German. Dr Klemperer's English is limited in construction and vocabulary and I think one reason for his agreement to a second series of conversations was his feeling that there were matters that he could better discuss in his native tongue. Perhaps, also, there were things, sometimes rather blunt things, that he wanted to say to a German audience.

In November 1969 I returned to Zürich for the WDR sessions to find that on the previous day Dr Klemperer had suffered one of his innumerable accidents. He had been taken for a drive by Mr Deszoe Ernster, the Hungarian bass, and, while getting out of the car to have a walk, he had fallen. Dr Klemperer is a man of formidable proportions and Mr Ernster had been unable to lift him until help had come half an hour later. When I arrived Dr Klemperer's face was bruised and bloody and he was visibly shaken. I urged that our conversations should be postponed. But with the extraordinary willpower which has carried him through a series of misadventures that would have crushed a lesser man, he insisted that we proceed as planned. There were moments when his voice grew alarmingly faint. Then some question would fire him and he would take new life. But I fear that those days were a considerable strain for a man of his years after a bad fall.

I must confess that they were not exactly a relaxation for me. We sat adjacent to each other in the sitting-room of his small and simply furnished flat, Dr Klemperer in his usual upright easy chair, with a lamp over his shoulder, stick on one side, pipes and books on the other. One detail in particular remains in my mind. Occasionally, we stopped so that I could confer with Miss Klemperer or the technician in charge of the recording apparatus in the other room. Whenever I returned, I found Dr Klemperer immersed in a book. Here, it seemed to me, was a man with those powers of sustained concentration that have become rare in an age of radio and television.

I had already had lunch with Dr Klemperer and his daughter on several occasions in London, and was less intimidated than I had been when I first found myself in the presence of this huge eagle of a man. I had learnt that one of the crucial elements in his complex character is modesty, that when he asks a question, it is because he wants an answer. He is plainly bored by conversation with a partner who cannot return the ball fairly smartly across the net. I had got to know, and enjoy, his humour, his pretence that he is a plaything in the hands of his daughter, his nurse, Schwester Ruth, and his housekeeper, Frau Anna, who take it in turn to care for him; his habit of making an outrageous assertion simply to test one's reaction, his laconic wit and peculiarly Jewish sense of irony. But, as countless orchestras have discovered, behind the banter there remains a dauntingly formidable figure who does not suffer fools gladly. I cannot say that I was at my ease as the first tape started to turn.

There were other difficulties. Dr Klemperer is a man of few words. When he has nothing to say, he says just that. Many of his answers were terse, even monosyllabic. Some amounted to little more than a grunt. As a result, readers may well feel some of his answers here to be perfunctory; so did I, but there was little I could do about it. Often information, particularly about his own achievements, had to be prised out of him. I was at that time unaware, for instance, that he had done more than any other man to make Janáček's operas known during his lifetime outside his native Czechoslovakia. Yet, because I put no questions, he made no reference to it. Nor did he tell me that he had himself been the producer of the first stage performance of Stravinsky's *Oedipus Rex*. Old men's memories of their early days are notoriously more vivid than those of more recent events. Bit by bit, however, I was able to piece together a fairly complete account of a career that stretches back to 1906, when Klemperer made his début as a conductor in a production by Max Reinhardt in Berlin of Offenbach's *Orpheus in the Underworld*.

In particular, I was anxious to draw him out on the many great composers with whom he has been connected. This was not because I was eager to cast him in the role of champion of contemporary music, though he has indeed been one. The significance of Klemperer's association with some of the outstanding creative figures of his time goes deeper than that. He is a representative of a fast vanishing age, in which the conductor had not yet sunk to the level of a mere virtuoso but was inextricably involved in the music of his own time, so that his sensibility and his technique developed out of a struggle to interpret it. Mahler's impact on Klemperer's life goes far deeper than the mere chance that it was he who recommended him for his first two appointments. Both as a man and a musician Mahler was a formative influence, and in a lesser degree the same is true of his association with Stravinsky and Schoenberg (Klemperer was one of the few musicians of his generation to champion the music of both composers, who for most of their lives were generally regarded as mutually exclusive). Would Klemperer's Beethoven have been the same had he not studied with Schoenberg and performed his music? Would the style of the Kroll Opera, over which he presided from 1927 to 1931, have marked such a decisive break with tradition, had he not been open to Stravinsky's anti-romantic aesthetic? I think that the answer to both those questions is no. That is why I have as far as possible put the names of composers with whom Klemperer has been associated at the head of the chapters in these printed conversations.

Programmes based on the tapes of the conversations were duly broadcast by CBC and WDR in May 1970, on the occasion of Dr Klemperer's eighty-fifth birthday. Naturally, these programmes represented only a small fraction of the taped material, so that when the CBC asked permission to reprint them in the form of a booklet, I began to wonder whether some attempt should not be made to present the conversations in a more complete form. Dr Klemperer is no writer. His small *Erinnerungen an Gustav Mahler*,[1] which with some additional material subsequently appeared in English with the title of *Minor Recollections*,[2] contains valuable information (some of which is inevitably duplicated in these conversations). But it is hardly more than a pamphlet, and, as Dr Klemperer has no intention of producing an autobiography, it seemed worthwhile to attempt something of a substitute for that by scrambling the English and the German conversations, both of which contain passages not in the other.

However well prepared, conversation inevitably meanders. Subjects are raised, dropped, returned to and discussed in different contexts, and in the struggle to produce from the English and German texts a reasonably coherent narrative I have unavoidably done violence to both versions. That was not the only cause for editorial intervention. Dr Klemperer's English has a flavour of its own, and, where possible, I have tried to preserve this. But it is one thing to *hear* someone use a language in an effective if unorthodox manner, and quite another to *read* it. The number of adjectives Dr Klemperer

[1] Atlantis Verlag, Zürich, 1960.   [2] Dennis Dobson, London, 1964.

uses in English is, for instance, limited. But spoken with the inflection of a voice that contains an altogether exceptional range of expression, is at times harsh, mocking or distant and at others caressing, quizzical or plaintive, that shortcoming is not as apparent as it would be in a written text.

I have therefore regretfully had to play the school-master and inflict "corrections" on the English original, and inevitably something has been lost in the process. The German text has also presented problems, simply because it is beyond my powers to translate Dr Klemperer's pungent and individual use of his native tongue into the sort of English he might himself speak. Again and again, my labours have drawn well justified protests from Lotte Klemperer ("but my father would never say that") and these have, I hope, served as a brake on my tendency to impose too literary a style. Certainly, Dr Klemperer is the least literary of men. His language is above all simple and direct (even if some of the underlying implications are not). Yet the mere need to reassemble and telescope material to avoid repetition, to produce language that reads easily, has inevitably imposed a certain infidelity on the original, to which I plead guilty in what I hope will be found mitigating circumstances. For instance, Dr Klemperer is not a man who speaks in long paragraphs, such as have emerged here simply because I have deleted questions that seem superfluous or repetitive and thus run together a series of brief replies. On the other hand I have let a number of contradictions stand. Walt Whitman's words

Do I contradict myself?
Very well then I contradict myself,
(I am large, I contain multitudes).

are as true of Otto Klemperer as of any man I have known.

I have also added a number of brief notes, where these have seemed necessary. But to avoid too weighty an apparatus, I have confined biographical details, where these are not essential to immediate understanding of the text, to the index. The reader may observe that occasional reference is made to events, such as Stravinsky's death and Dr Klemperer's retirement in 1972 from public concert-giving, that occurred after the original conversations took place. These were added on a subsequent visit to Zürich, when Dr Klemperer checked the written version.

There is perhaps another matter that calls for comment. If the subject of German persecution of the Jews runs through these conversations with the persistence of a *Leitmotiv*, it has to be remembered that many of the men with whom Klemperer has been most closely associated died or had a large part of their lives ruined as a result of anti-Semitic policies of the Nazis. Klemperer himself was forty-eight when Hitler became Chancellor in 1933. He was at the height of his powers, generally acknowledged as one of the two or three outstanding conductors of his generation and admired above all as an interpreter of German music. It was for his services in this field that he was awarded the Goethe Medal (a rare honour) in the very year in which he was obliged to flee his native land. Had he been less profoundly German in his sensibilities and up-bringing, a better example of the rootless, cosmopolitan Jew dear to Nazi imagination, America might have proved a less alien world. Had he been less the child of what before 1933 was widely supposed to be a liberal and humanistic age, the shock of finding himself a victim of racial persecution might have been less great. As it was, he was condemned to twenty-one years of exile. He was obliged to wander with his family in strange lands, often ill and sometimes poor. No doubt the immense fame and success that have come to him in the evening of his life have provided some compensation for these sufferings. But, as these conversations amply confirm, the memory of those years is a wound that will never close.

*   *   *

I would particularly like to express my thanks to Miss Lotte Klemperer, without whose support and advice these conversations would not have been published; to Mr Philo Bregstein who has most generously allowed me to include several passages from an interview he had with Dr Klemperer; to Mr Robert Chesterman, who presided over the CBC sessions with unfailing tact and good-humour; to Dr Wolfgang Seifert of WDR, Cologne, who was the instigator of the German conversations; to Deutschlandfunk for permission to include a few brief extracts from an interview Dr Klemperer gave to Herr Ernst-Ludwig Gausmann; to Mr Harold Rosenthal, who generously provided information for notes that I could not find elsewhere; and to Frau Anna Hesch, whose succulent and aromatic *Sauerbraten* taught me that it need not be the greasy stew with a sour taste one is liable to encounter in German restaurants.

Above all, I owe a deep debt to Dr Klemperer, who suffered my questionings with patience and good-humour. No man has done more to extend my understanding of the world of the great classics from Haydn to Mahler. This small book is, in some sense, an act of homage and a labour of love.

London,
6 June 1972.

B

CONVERSATIONS WITH KLEMPERER

CHAPTER I

Early Memories

HEYWORTH: Dr Klemperer, you were born in Germany. But am I right in supposing that your origins are Austrian rather than German?

KLEMPERER: My father was born in Prague, where my grandfather, who was a teacher of religion, lies buried. So we belonged absolutely to the Austro-Hungarian monarchy. The name Klemperer was originally Klopper. Formerly, a member of the Jewish community had to wake people up so that they got to the synagogue on time. He was called the *Klopper* because he knocked[1] on the doors. My great-great-grandfather was born in 1758 as Gumpel Klopper and was buried forty-five years later in 1803 as Marcus Klemperer.

I didn't know my grandfather, but he is said to have been very strict and orthodox. He had five children, of whom my father, Nathan, was one. My father had a good voice and recited splendidly from the German classics, especially Goethe and Schiller. But in spite of his talent, he couldn't become an artist, because my grandfather could only afford to pay for one of his four sons to study. So he went into his brother's doll business in Breslau.

My father met my mother there at a trade fair for dolls. In 1881 they married and settled in Breslau, where I was born in 1885. The marriage, which was basically a good one, was a mixture of Ashkenasi and Sephardic blood. The Rée family originally came from Spain. After the famous expulsion of the Jews in 1492 they went to France and probably moved at the time of St Bartholomew's Night[2] to Altona,[3] which was then Danish. Later they finally settled in Hamburg. Eventually there was a quarrel between my father and his brother, so in 1889 my parents decided to move to Hamburg, where they could rely on help from my mother's family, who were well off. It is a good custom among Jews that they help one another. But my father was more interested in Schubert and Schiller

[1] *Klopfte.*
[2] Massacre of the French Protestants in 1572, which set off the Huguenot emigration.
[3] Today a suburb of Hamburg.

than keeping the books of a business, so that financially things didn't go well. Originally, he wanted to set up a steam laundry, but he didn't have the capital. There were difficult years in which my father earned practically nothing and relations helped. Finally he found a job as manager of a stocking business, something that he knew absolutely nothing about. Then for a few years things went better, until he lost his job. So it went on, up and down. Sometimes he had a small income, sometimes nothing at all. He was a wretched business man, but he had real artistic gifts.

My parents had really got to know each other through music. My father sang Schubert, Loewe, Mozart, Schumann and Brahms and my mother, who was a professional piano teacher, accompanied and coached him, because he couldn't read a note, but sung everything by ear. My first musical memory is of my father singing, especially *Dichterliebe*. I've always loved Schumann and even today I'm always pleased when I can conduct one of his symphonies.

HEYWORTH: Do you have any other memories from your earliest years in Breslau?

KLEMPERER: I have only one vivid memory. One afternoon on a walk a big, black dog jumped on my shoulders. Since then I have always been frightened of dogs. Again and again, in various forms I have seen a black dog or a black man and that has never been a good omen for me.

HEYWORTH: How old were you when you left Breslau?

KLEMPERER: We left when I was four and a half. In Hamburg the first thing I saw from the train were the round pillars with concert and theatre advertisements. They fascinated me, and what a role they have played in my life! I lived in Hamburg until I was sixteen and I feel myself absolutely a Hamburger.

Our apartment there faced a big field, where cows grazed, and we used to drink the raw milk from their udders. That was the scene of my first "crime". I didn't like going to school and I was a careless pupil, and in this field I buried a bad school report. It didn't help as a duplicate was sent to my parents.

My form-master wrote in my school book, "Wer etwas kann, den hält man wert, den Ungeschickten niemand begehrt."[1] I was very clumsy. Sometimes I fell and dirtied my clothes, and when I got home I got into trouble. From my earliest days I always tried to avoid anything unpleasant. I didn't like being reproached. So I invented a lie. I told my parents that a big man with a black beard had followed me and pushed me on to the ground, and that I only had escaped by running away. My parents believed it, and my mother even went to the police.

I often told this lie. But I was quite clear that I was doing something very wrong. I thought, "It's terrible that I am always lying," though that didn't stop me from continuing to do so. Then in an illustrated magazine I saw a picture of a man

[1] Literally, "He who can do something, the world values; no one envies the clumsy man".

making a confession on his deathbed, and I thought it will be the same with me. Finally, I couldn't bear it any more, and one evening—I was already in bed—I ran down to the living-room and told my parents everything. They didn't believe me. They laughed and said, "Oh you're tired. Go back to bed and we'll talk about it tomorrow." But next morning, I stuck to what I had told them, and when I finally said that as punishment I wouldn't go on holiday that summer, then they believed me. And so it turned out. My mother went away with my sisters and I stayed at home with my father.

But at the end of that summer my father and I went for a week to Holstein. We were supposed to go on foot; my father had promised my mother that on account of money difficulties. But of course it turned out differently. We took the train to Eutin, stayed in a very nice hotel and generally gave ourselves a good time. In the evening my father sang and I accompanied him on the piano. Some of the guests were delighted and thought that we were "travelling artists", who had been engaged. It was a lovely week. But the memory of that black dog which jumped on my shoulders when I was very small in Breslau remained with me for many years.

HEYWORTH: You mean that the black dog and the black man were linked in your imagination?

KLEMPERER: Yes, absolutely. After the "crime" I determined that nothing like that must happen again and I became a good pupil. I said to myself, "Now I've finished with such things."[1] But, you understand, it stayed on my conscience for many years that I had not told the truth. I was obsessed by it.

At the age of about thirteen, I went to the *Realgymnasium* of the Johanneum which is one of the oldest schools in Hamburg. The *Realgymnasium* is a grammar school, where Greek isn't taught, only Latin and modern languages. They came to me easily. But mathematics were a torment, so here I just cheated. One class I shall never forget. There was a deputy master, and he said that, as he hadn't prepared what we were supposed to learn, he would read to us. He read Mark Antony's speech from Shakespeare's *Julius Caesar*. The impression it made on me was overwhelming.

For the most part the masters were very nice. But I was always second in the class. I couldn't be first: that wouldn't have been possible. That would have gone against the general trend.

HEYWORTH: I don't quite understand.

KLEMPERER: I was the second. My marks were often better than those of the first. But I was not the first.

HEYWORTH: And why?

KLEMPERER: Anti-Semitism! Because one didn't put a Jew at the head of a class in a

[1] Klemperer was about eight years old at the time.

great German *Gymnasium*. Yes, without a doubt. In one lesson there was French discussion. So you could only speak in French. That was the time of the so-called *Flottenvorlage*.[1] My father, who was an old-fashioned liberal, complained bitterly that this bill should ever have been put before the Reichstag. During the lesson the teacher and the class discussed the question. So I stood up and said, "Mais la flotte coutera beaucoup d'argent et le peuple doit payer." You can't imagine what happened then. They all shouted "socialist" at me. But the master said to the class, "I don't understand what you are shouting at. Grammatically, that was absolutely right." *Echt Deutsch!*

Another example. On September 2[2] the school always made an outing to Bismarck's grave at Friedrichsruh.[3] One boy carried the flag and another the so-called class emblem. I wasn't allowed to carry either. That wasn't possible.

We had a drawing class and we had to draw a little cube in front of us. Well, the master came, and once again I hadn't got it right. I said, "You know, I just can't draw a straight line." He said, "No wonder in view of your race." Anti-Semitism, my God, it was always there. Napoleon ordered a complete integration of the Jews in Germany. But once he was defeated, reaction returned to Prussia and Austria and with it anti-Semitism became even stronger than it had been before. Germany became a police state and the 1848 revolution did nothing to change that.

HEYWORTH: What are your earliest musical memories?

KLEMPERER: If I remember rightly, my first artistic impression wasn't musical at all. It was Schiller's *Wilhelm Tell*, and in the apple scene I broke into such noisy sobs that my mother had to take me out of the theatre. I was about eight or nine at the time. My parents subscribed every year to a Schiller cycle and my sisters and I took it in turns to go. I also went to the opera. I remember what an impact *Fidelio* had on me when I was about thirteen. It was above all the canon[4] in the first act that made a deep impression on me. And *Il Trovatore*; I found that splendid. Apparently I had no understanding of Mozart. I still remember that *Don Giovanni* passed over me without having much effect. Then, when I was about fifteen, my mother took me to a concert at which Strauss's *Tod und Verklärung* was performed for the first time in Hamburg. That impressed me tremendously; the sound of the orchestra, the whole build-up—I found it wonderful.

HEYWORTH: When did your musical education begin?

KLEMPERER: From quite early it was the intention that I should be a musician. I had piano lessons from my mother and at the age of six I already played quite nicely.

---

[1] A Parliamentary bill to increase the size of the German Navy.
[2] Anniversary of the victory over the French at Sedan in 1870.
[3] His country estate near Hamburg at which he died in 1898.
[4] The quartet, *Mir is so wunderbar*.

But I was very difficult and always knew better. "No," I said, "I want it like this." So I got another teacher, Herr Havekoss, and I learnt a lot with him. Until I was fifteen I had lessons every week and studied Bach's Inventions and went on up to Beethoven sonatas, chamber music and so on. From then on I practised for two hours every day.

I must have shown some special talent for music quite early. One day in Hamburg, when I was about seven or eight, I went to the Zoological Gardens to listen to a military band. I stood behind a clarinettist, looked at his music and noticed that he was playing different notes. I asked him why, and he laughed and said, "But it's a B flat clarinet".[1] He was right, of course, but he was surprised that I had noticed.

One day a cousin of my mother, Frau Helene Rée, visited us and found only me at home. She was very impressed by my piano-playing and told my mother that she would pay for my whole musical education, which my parents weren't in a position to do. But to myself I thought, when I'm free, I'll become an actor: that was my great wish. It has never been fulfilled, though something of this desire has always remained.

To decide whether I had enough talent to become a musician, in 1900 a friend of my mother's came to examine me. He was Mr Max Mayer,[2] a German pianist who lived in Manchester. I remember I played for him sonatas by Philipp Emanuel Bach and Beethoven. He then tested my ear and he asked me whether I had written anything, and I had. I played a little piece for him, very childish, and he said, "Well, that's not very important." But then he said to my mother, "I cannot say that your son will be a Hans Richter, but I am sure he can become a good musician." And so it was decided. But I remember particularly the seriousness with which he told me that success should never be decisive in a musician's life; the essential thing was inner satisfaction, even if outward success didn't come.

My mother had taken me to a concert given in Hamburg by a Dutch pianist, James Kwast, and it was decided that I should go to study with him at the Hoch Conservatory in Frankfurt. So I never took my *Abitur*.[3] But I was overjoyed to have got away from school. That summer of 1901 was one of the happiest of my life. I devoured books—Halbe, Sudermann, Hartleben and Schnitzler—and learnt a lot from them. Then at the end of August my mother took me to Frankfurt, where I lived with an old piano teacher, and after an exam I was accepted by the conservatory. So came the day of freedom.

[1] A transposing instrument on which the music sounds a tone lower than it is notated. The story indicates that Klemperer had perfect pitch at an unusually early age.
[2] Professor of piano at the Royal Manchester College of Music 1908–1924.
[3] Examination, roughly equivalent of "A" levels.

Kwast was no Leschetizky,[1] who was more concerned with technique. But he was a splendid musician. I also learnt to play the violin a little and I studied theory with Ivan Knorr.[2] To Kwast and Knorr I owe the basis of my musical development. Frankfurt delighted me. First of all I was glad to be on my own, and then I heard a lot of opera and concerts. As music students we had the right to go to final rehearsals without paying. There I heard both Eugen D'Albert and Paderewski. Especially D'Albert, who played Beethoven's Fifth Concerto, seemed to me splendid. And there I heard *The Ring* for the first time.

HEYWORTH: Were you a keen Wagnerian?

KLEMPERER: Immensely. In the first place I was enormously interested in the text. I took Wagner very seriously. I mean, I considered him Beethoven's successor. Heavens, I was sixteen. I had been brought up on Mozart, Beethoven and Schubert: I knew nothing. I was given the Grieg Piano Concerto to play and it sounded terribly modern.

HEYWORTH: You were keener on Wagner than Brahms?[3]

KLEMPERER: At first, yes. But that changed with time. A bit later, in the course of my piano studies in Berlin, I felt myself very much drawn to Brahms. Then, still later, at the beginning of the 1914–1918 war, I was working with Pfitzner as a conductor in Strasbourg. As you know, he was a great Wagnerian and he brought me back to Wagner to some extent.

But my greatest impression in Frankfurt was the famous singer Stockhausen.[4] He gave classes and, I don't know why, I was asked to accompany. But he had some very untalented pupils. One of them sang Schumann's song, *Du Ring an meinem Finger*, and he said, "It's terrible, the way you sing. Herr Klemperer, please play simply the melody on the piano." I did so, and then he said, "You see, that's how it should sound." Oh, I was tremendously proud.

My life in Frankfurt was very regular. I practised the piano for eight hours every day and the violin for one; then for another hour I did theory exercises. I enjoyed my ten hour day. My first appearance in a conservatory concert was a big event for me. I played Beethoven's D major sonata, Opus 10, and the intense

[1] Theodor Leschetizky (1830–1915). Famous teacher of a whole generation of pianists, including Paderewski.

[2] 1853–1917. Professor of composition, and subsequently director of the Hoch Conservatory, where he was the teacher of the English "Frankfurt school" of Cyril Scott, Roger Quilter and Balfour Gardiner.

[3] These were years when musical life in Central Europe was still divided between the Wagnerians and the Brahmins.

[4] Julius Stockhausen (1826–1906). German baritone, especially renowned for his Lieder singing. It has been said that Stockhausen "was to Brahms's songs very much what Joachim was to his chamber music".

nervousness I felt beforehand disappeared when I started to play. Unfortunately, later it never left me.

After only a year my teacher Kwast left Frankfurt because of a love affair and a divorce, and I went with him to Berlin where he had a post at the Klindworth-Scharwenka Conservatory. I didn't like Berlin at all. Compared to the impressive Hoch Conservatory in Frankfurt it was all very small. But I had pretty good teachers. I studied the piano intensely, also theory with Phillip Scharwenka, to whom I owe a great deal. And then I had score reading with Berger. That was also very good. He was a well-known composer at that time, and he also conducted the Meiningen orchestra as assistant to Steinbach. In 1905 Kwast went to the Stern Conservatory, which ranked far higher than the Klindworth-Scharwenka, and there I had composition and conducting lessons with Hans Pfitzner.[1]

Of course I went to a lot of concerts in Berlin. I particularly remember one at the former Künstlerhaus, near Potsdamer Platz, where Johannes Messchaert sang an entire programme of Mahler songs, accompanied by Mahler himself. Messchaert didn't have a large voice, but it was extraordinarily expressive. He was really the Josef Joachim of the voice—nothing less. His singing in Bach cantatas was indescribable. But on this particular occasion the hall was half empty. It was in 1906 and people didn't yet know who Mahler was. They only knew that he came from Vienna, and at that time that was a long way away.

I also heard Busoni and Max Reger, who was a splendid pianist. But the greatest non-musical impression of my student days in Berlin were Max Reinhardt's productions. He really brought life into the theatre, because at that time the Koenigliches Schauspielhaus[2] was terrible. Reinhardt had started life as an actor—a very good actor. He nearly always played old men. Then he became director of the Neues Theater, which today is called Theater am Schiffbauerdamm, the Brecht Theatre. There he produced *A Midsummer Night's Dream* with Mendelssohn's music. That was wonderful. And he gave *Pelléas et Mélisande*—Maeterlinck's play—and Oscar Wilde's *Salome* and German classics. His lighting was really magical. And his actors—Moissi as Oberon: wonderful. Then he became director of the Deutsches Theater. But later he went in for spectacle, like doing the *Oresteia* in a circus. He made a lot of money, but artistically it was a decline. He did dozens of productions of *A Midsummer Night's Dream*, in London and Los Angeles and other places, but never so well as in Berlin. That freshness had gone. After 1933 he went to America, but he didn't have much success there. You see the Americans thought, oh, Max Reinhardt will bring a new sort of theatre. But

[1] 1869–1949. Composer who in Germany during his lifetime ranked as a conservative counterpart to his contemporary, Richard Strauss. See Chapter 3. Pfitzner had eloped with the daughter of James Kwast and married her in London.
[2] The official state-subsidised theatre.

he didn't. He belonged to the old romantic theatre and did it very well. But he wasn't an innovator.

Well, I really had many interests. Yet when I look back on my time in Berlin, it is a pity that I didn't have any mentor who would have been responsible for my extra-musical development. I could have gone to lectures at the University and things like that. But no one made me aware of them and so I didn't go. I just practised the piano eight hours a day.

HEYWORTH: You had a marked talent for the piano?

KLEMPERER: It seemed so. But it was difficult to find a room where I could practise undisturbed. For some time I had an attic in Frankfurt. But the people complained: they said, we don't want to hear this noisy piano. And then in Berlin there was the same difficulty. But somehow I got through. At the Klindworth-Scharwenka Conservatory there was a prize of 200 marks for the best piano pupil. I played Bach's Chromatic Fantasia and Fugue and I got the prize.

In 1905 Kwast put me in for the Rubinstein competition in Paris, which was really nonsense as I wasn't advanced enough to compete. There were two prizes, one for pianists, the other for composers—each, I think, for 5,000 francs. Backhaus won the piano prize. Bartók also took part and played a work of his own for the composition prize. He didn't get it. It was decided to give no prize for composition that year, as in the jury's opinion no one was worthy of it! Later, in September 1905, I entered for the Mendelssohn prize in Berlin and Joachim was on the jury. I played the Hammerklavier sonata and after the adagio Joachim said, "Well, we don't need to hear the last movement." But Rudorff,[1] who was also on the jury, said, "I think now that the young man has played the first three movements we should let him play the finale." And so I did. But the prize was given to a singer, whom I never heard of afterwards. Never. I can still remember her name: Fräulein Martik. But at least I was commended.

I used to hear Joachim when he rehearsed with his quartet on the morning of their concerts in the Singakademie. Enormous. I mean, he played like a Hungarian musician with a lot of temperament—not like the director of the music academy, which he was.

HEYWORTH: Why did you give up the piano? And how did you become a conductor?

KLEMPERER: I was always so nervous that my hands became wet. James Kwast said to me, "You always play much better at lessons than in public. You are not the same in public." And he was right. But I didn't give up the piano; I worked as a pianist and accompanist for a number of years. My first conducting engagement happened by accident. For some time I had worked as accompanist at rehearsals of the Stern'sche Gesangverein, one of the big Berlin choirs, and in this way I had

[1] Ernst Rudorff (1840–1916). Pianist and teacher.

got to know Oscar Fried, who was its conductor. Originally he had been a horn player, but he had studied musical theory and worked his way up to being a conductor. In the meantime he earned his living as a dog breeder. He lived from that, but he also got a lot of pleasure from it. He became conductor of the Stern'sche Gesangverein, and the first thing he did was Liszt's *Die heilige Elisabeth*, which was still hardly known in Berlin. Then he did some Mahler symphonies, and the success was so immense that he founded a society for new music in Berlin. At that time Berlin was not nearly as open to new music as it became in the twenties. I had a very good impression of Fried as a conductor. But, though he achieved a great deal, his career never really developed. In 1933 he had to leave Germany. He went to Russia, married a Russian and died there during the last war.

In 1906 Fried wrote to tell me that Max Reinhardt was planning to produce Offenbach's *Orpheus in the Underworld* at the Neues Theater, but that he hardly knew the work and wanted to hear it. So I played it to him and after I had done so I was engaged as chorus master and deputy-director. The rehearsals lasted a long time, but I felt at home in that atmosphere of the theatre with great actors like Tilla Durieux, Georg Engels and Moissi and Hans Wassmann, who were all in the cast. Reinhardt did *Orpheus* with actors, not singers. But they could all sing well. In particular, Moissi had a wonderfully expressive voice.

After the second performance there was a terrible fight between Fried and the soprano. So I took over. It was a great moment for me when Max Reinhardt said, "All right, then we'll take Klemperer." I mean, he had confidence that I could do it. I conducted *Orpheus* fifty times—a very amusing occupation.

CHAPTER II

Mahler and the Start of a Career

HEYWORTH: Didn't you see Mahler in the street as a small boy in Hamburg?

KLEMPERER: Oh yes! You see, we lived in West Hamburg and Mahler lived there also, and so I used to see him on my way to school. I saw a man who limped a little. I don't know how, but I knew it was the Kapellmeister Mahler. Probably it was because he was then conductor at the opera[1] and my parents often went and brought back the programme, so that I was very much aware of his name from my early childhood.

But it was Schwarwenka in Berlin who first told me that he was a great composer. That was about 1903 or 1904, and at that time I didn't know any of his music. Shortly afterwards, Nikisch gave a performance of the Fifth Symphony and I heard it. But I was very disappointed.

HEYWORTH: When did you first meet Mahler?

KLEMPERER: I met him twice in Berlin. The first time was in 1905 when Fried was conducting his Second Symphony and asked me to conduct the off-stage orchestra. Mahler came to the last rehearsal, and afterwards I went to him and asked, "Excuse me, but was it all right?" He said, "No, it was terrible. It was too loud. It should sound very quietly from behind." I said, "But it says *sehr schmetternd*[2] in the score." He replied, "But from a long way away; it was much too close." It wasn't possible to get that far away, so I said to the musicians, "Play it *piano*: the whole thing." They did so and the performance was an enormous success. Mahler embraced Fried on the stage and when he came into the artists' room he shook my hand and said, "Very good." I was proud.

Then that same winter he came again to Berlin and himself conducted his Third Symphony. That was the first time I heard him rehearse. I saw how he conducted: it was very, very good. Even Pfitzner, who was not at all a friend of Mahler's music, said, "He is a colossal conductor."

[1] 1891–1897.   [2] Literally, "very blaring".

At that time Mahler was staying a long way from the Philharmonie[1] and he asked, "Where is the Augsburgerstrasse?" I said, "If you will allow me, I will accompany you." I went with him on the elevated railway—it was absolutely new, but he was not interested in such things. He said to me, "You are composing?" I said, "No, I couldn't call my works compositions." "Yes, yes," he said. "I can see that you compose." Again, I was very proud.

HEYWORTH: Did he look at your compositions?

KLEMPERER: No, no, not at all, only at my face.

HEYWORTH: What was so remarkable about him as a conductor?

KLEMPERER: It's very difficult to say. His tempi—one felt they could not have been otherwise. When he was younger, he is said to have conducted with enormous passion. I heard him only a few years before his death, and then he was very economical in his movements, though not so economical as Richard Strauss. He had been told[2] by doctors that he had a bad heart and so he was very careful.

HEYWORTH: If we heard Mahler conduct today would we feel his performances to be very romantic?

KLEMPERER: No, no, no. Toscanini was the greatest conductor of his generation, but Mahler was a hundred times greater. I mean, Toscanini's performances, and especially his Beethoven, were sometimes very disputable. But Mahler, never. I heard him several times. The first time was at the Vienna Opera in the second and third acts of *Die Walküre*, and then in concerts in Prague, where he conducted a number of things, including the *Meistersinger* prelude, the overture to *The Bartered Bride* and Beethoven's Seventh Symphony. It was phenomenal. For me there was only one thought—to give up this profession, if one couldn't conduct like that.

HEYWORTH: Were his tempi strict in the classics?

KLEMPERER: Very strict. I can only repeat: everything was absolutely natural.[3] It had to be like that. One heard and said, "Yes, of course, it's right." I still remember the opening of the second movement of Beethoven's Seventh Symphony: it sounded quite different, but I could absolutely say "yes" to it. When he conducted you felt it couldn't be better and it couldn't be otherwise. That isn't the case with other conductors: with one you have this reservation, with another that, but you don't feel completely comfortable. With Mahler never.

HEYWORTH: Did he make a great impact in the theatre?

KLEMPERER: Very great. Apart from *Die Walküre*, I had the good luck to hear Gluck's *Iphigenia in Aulis*, and in that, incidentally, he was his own producer. There was a producer to carry out his instructions, but he was the *spiritus rector*

[1] Concert hall of the Berlin Philharmonic Orchestra, which Mahler was conducting.

[2] Summer 1907.   [3] Original: "selbstverständlich".

of the whole thing. Of course he worked very closely with Roller[1] as designer. All his later productions—*Figaro, Don Giovanni, Das Rheingold, Die Walküre* (he left Vienna before he could complete *The Ring*) and *Iphigenia in Aulis*—were done with Roller. I remember during a rehearsal there was no more work to be done with the orchestra and he sat in the theatre with Walter, Roller and other people who worked with him. During a chorus he turned to Roller and asked whether it wouldn't be better to add a ballet. That I remember clearly. And he accompanied wonderfully: there was complete unity. Gutheil-Schoder was Iphigenie. Enchanting.

Die Walküre was especially fine. I've never heard the fight between Siegmund and Hunding so clear and transparent, and those fresh Viennese voices, ah, they were excellent. Mildenburg sang Brünnhilde, Schmedes was Siegmund. Wonderful, wonderful.

HEYWORTH: Was Mahler not also conductor of the Vienna Philharmonic Orchestra?

KLEMPERER: Yes, but only for three seasons.[1] He demanded many rehearsals and the Philharmonic Orchestra doesn't like that. Instead of Mahler, they took Hellmesberger, who was a very unimportant musician. Mahler conducted relatively few concerts in Europe. Later, when he was speaking about his period in New York[2] and I asked him what he liked best in America, he said, "I can tell you that the greatest experience I had there was conducting Beethoven's Pastoral Symphony." Imagine, a man of fifty with his reputation, and no orchestra in Germany or Austria gave him the chance to conduct the Pastoral Symphony! New York was the first place in which he had his own orchestra and could do what he wanted.

HEYWORTH: Was he happy in New York?

KLEMPERER: God knows, not! I mean, no one understood him. No one had an idea of who he was. At first he was at the opera. Alfred Hertz, who worked there, was at Mahler's first *Tristan* rehearsal.[3] He told me that Mahler didn't say a word. Only at the end he suddenly said, "The entry of the main motif, the trumpets stronger: one must hear the crescendo." And through that single remark the entire prelude was transformed. But then already in his second year in New York he didn't conduct at the Metropolitan, because Gatti-Casazza[4] had engaged Toscanini from Milan. Toscanini had said that he would only come if his first opera was *Tristan*. It was at the time when Mahler himself had just conducted *Tristan*, and it was strange to have perhaps another sixteen to twenty rehearsals. But Mahler himself went to Toscanini's performance. His wife later told me

[1] 1898–1901.
[2] Mahler was appointed conductor of the newly founded Philharmonic Society in 1909.
[3] Mahler made his debut at the Metropolitan Opera with *Tristan und Isolde* on 1 January 1908.
[4] Giulio Gatti-Casazza (1869–1940). Italian opera manager who was general manager of the Metropolitan Opera 1908–1935.

a and *b*   About 1905
c   With his sister Marianne at Westerland in 1908
d   Hamburg, 1910
e   Strasbourg, 1915

In the opera pit at Strasbourg, 1915

that he said, "It isn't our *Tristan*, but this conductor knows what he wants."

HEYWORTH: Your own enthusiasm for Mahler's music dates from that performance of the Second Symphony you took part in in Berlin in 1905?

KLEMPERER: Yes. Today I like his *Kindertotenlieder* and the *Lieder eines fahrenden Gesellen* and some of the symphonies. But not all of them. I mean, I am not a stupid, enthusiastic boy: I don't like everything he wrote. The First Symphony I have only conducted once in my life and I don't like the last movement at all. In the Fifth I very much like the first movement, the Funeral March. But the scherzo is for me too long. And then the adagietto—the little piece for harp and strings—that's very nice, but it comes close to salon music. The last movement is also too long. And so I've never conducted the symphony.

HEYWORTH: You've never conducted the Sixth, either.

KLEMPERER: I know. I played the celesta at a performance conducted by Oscar Fried in Berlin, and I think Mahler was present; yes, he was. It's a great work. The last movement is really a cosmos in itself; it's tragic synthesis of life and death. But I must honestly say that I don't understand it. And I think that the second theme of the first movement is highly questionable. It's a very complicated work. Mahler was very moved by it; he felt that he had written it for himself.

HEYWORTH: Which of Mahler's symphonies do you think is the greatest?

KLEMPERER: I think the Ninth is the greatest, greater for my taste than the Eighth. I conducted it several times in the twenties, when Mahler still wasn't much performed. And then again in London and elsewhere in 1967 and 1968, and in Israel in 1970. The festival there wanted the Fourth. But I've done that so often and I wanted to do something harder, just to show people what the Jerusalem radio orchestra can do. I haven't conducted there often, but I love that old land.

HEYWORTH: What do you feel about using a baritone in *Das Lied von der Erde*? At Edinburgh you conducted it with Fischer-Dieskau. But in your recording the soloist is Christa Ludwig.

KLEMPERER: I think a contralto is much better. Although Mahler himself suggested it, I find that the piece sounds monotonous with two men's voices, and God knows it isn't that.

HEYWORTH: Is that the only occasion you have used a baritone?

KLEMPERER: No. In Cologne in the early twenties I did it with Friedrich Schorr. But parts of it lie too high for a baritone. I also did *Das Lied von der Erde* with Kathleen Ferrier. That was wonderful.

HEYWORTH: Weren't you at Mahler's own rehearsals for the first performances of his Seventh and Eighth Symphonies?

KLEMPERER: Yes. I heard the first performance of the Seventh in Prague in 1909. Each day after the rehearsals he took all the parts back with him to his hotel and

C

made improvements. There were a lot of young people there and we wanted to help him. But he wouldn't let us. He trusted no one.

HEYWORTH: Isn't it strange that a composer of his calibre was always altering his scores even in rehearsal?

KLEMPERER: Of course, it *is* strange. But it was part of his nature. He was always searching. He was never satisfied. In 1910 I went to Munich to hear rehearsals for his Eighth Symphony. I couldn't go to the performance itself, as I was conducting *Lohengrin* in Hamburg.[1] The soloists and the orchestra were there, but not the choir. Even so, it was wonderful. I must say that for the first time I felt that I was in the presence of a great composer. But he was still not satisfied with the scoring. During rehearsals he kept making small changes. He would say, "No, take this for two clarinets, or this alone, or this louder or softer." Some years before he died, he said, "The trouble is I cannot orchestrate." He was never satisfied. He always wanted more clarity, more sound, more dynamic contrast. At one point during the rehearsals for the Eighth Symphony he turned to some of us in the auditorium and said, "If, after my death, something doesn't sound right, then change it. You have not only the right but the duty to do so."

Those are good words for people who believe a conductor should never touch the notes. All this talk that one shouldn't change a single note in a score is nonsense. *Werktreue*, that is, faithfulness to the work, is a very different matter from merely using the pure text, isn't it? In my opinion, Wagner's retouchings of Beethoven's Ninth sometimes go *too* far, especially in the scherzo, where the second theme is scored for woodwind only and he added horns. Through them the whole movement takes on a sensuous character it doesn't really have. And Mahler went further. He made a number of retouchings in the Beethoven Symphonies and some of them are very bold. I've seen his score of the Ninth, though I've never performed it.

But one must never forget that Mahler explicitly said, "These retouchings I have made for myself, not for anyone else. When I conduct, I can take responsibility for them." And I can tell you his personality was such that when he conducted, one didn't feel them as retouchings. Some of those in the Seventh Symphony for instance, are, I believe, wrong. There was a tremendous scandal when he performed it in Vienna. It went around that Mahler had "improved" Beethoven. Mahler had a leaflet distributed to the audience, in which he explained that he had not tried to improve Beethoven; he had tried to do what Wagner has already done, only he had gone a little further. But it was all in vain. The public was furious. To touch "their" Beethoven—actually, Beethoven wasn't born in Vienna—that was sacrilege.

HEYWORTH: And you, what retouchings do you make?

[1] See page 40.

KLEMPERER: I don't do as much as Mahler did, and then only where I find it absolutely necessary. But in some passages, it is; if only because, for instance, there were in Beethoven's day no valves in horns and trumpets. Everything had to be played on a natural brass instrument which must have sounded terrible. Then again, where there is a melody or a melodic theme in the first violins which I want to bring out, I also give it to the second violins, and the second violin parts I give to some of the violas, so that it is still there. In the Eighth Symphony, in the first movement, there is a passage on the 'celli and the basses, where all the other instruments have only harmony, and I add four horns, and that sounds very well. Then in the funeral march of the Eroica, I begin with eight violins and use all sixteen only later. In this whole business of retouching, my motto is, "Sehe jeder, wie er's treibe."[1]

HEYWORTH: What about repeats?

KLEMPERER: One must repeat.

HEYWORTH: In all cases?

KLEMPERER: No, but in the Ninth one must.

HEYWORTH: What about the first movement of the Fifth?

KLEMPERER: Yes, one must. I haven't always done so. But now I would. I remember a discussion with Erich Korngold. He said, "The opening of the first movement, that cannot come twice." That influenced me and for some years I didn't make a repeat. But now I do. And in the last movement of the Jupiter Symphony, there one must repeat, though many people don't do so.

HEYWORTH: But what about Mahler's versions of the Schumann symphonies, where he not only retouched, but cut?

KLEMPERER: My goodness, those he made for himself. That they were published was just financial. After his death his widow, Alma, sold his versions to Universal Edition.

HEYWORTH: Do you make retouchings in Schumann?

KLEMPERER: Yes, though I don't go as far as Mahler. There are some things one absolutely must alter.

HEYWORTH: What about Deryck Cooke's realisation of Mahler's Tenth Symphony?

KLEMPERER: A scandal. Mahler told his wife to burn the sketches in the event of his death. She didn't do so. Apart from the adagio, which I have conducted, there is nothing more than sketches, sometimes only a single line of a few notes. When I heard that a man called Cooke had completed them, I asked for a score. It's impossible. I mean, if Cooke were a second Mahler, then it might be all right.

HEYWORTH: Do you think Mahler was religious, or merely had a longing to be religious?

KLEMPERER: No, he was religious. He was absolutely religious, only not a believer

[1] Quotation from Goethe's *Beherzigung*. Literally, "Let each one see for himself how he does it."

in dogma. He was born a Jew and he was baptised by the time he was in Hamburg. To become director of the Vienna Court Opera[1] it was absolutely necessary to be a Catholic. But he was never a Catholic in a dogmatic sense.

HEYWORTH: What was Mahler like?

KLEMPERER: Physically, he was very small. There were two sides to his nature. On the one hand there was an enormous energy. He was absolutely unwilling to make concessions. On the other hand he could be very *gemütlich*. I remember that after the afternoon rehearsals for his Seventh Symphony in Prague, many friends went back with him to his hotel and then he spoke very freely. I remember him saying, "My successor in Vienna, Mr Weingartner, naturally hates me. But he also hates Wagner, because now he makes cuts in *Die Walküre* and *Siegfried*". And that was really not good because cuts make a work longer, not shorter. Don't you agree? And then he spoke angrily about Hugo Wolf. I was very surprised: they were both from Vienna and the same age.[2] I told him I thought that Wolf was a great composer. Mahler looked angry, so I said, "Forgive me, that's only my opinion." But all in all, those afternoons were very relaxed and enjoyable.

[1] Mahler was appointed director of the Vienna Court Opera in 1897 and remained in this position until 1907.

[2] Wolf, like Mahler, was born in 1860. As students in Vienna the two composers had shared lodgings.

CHAPTER III

Strauss, Pfitzner and the German Provinces

HEYWORTH: It was through Mahler that you got your first appointment as a conductor, wasn't it?

KLEMPERER: Yes. I was still at conservatory while I was conducting those performances of *Orpheus in the Underworld* for Reinhardt in 1906. Afterwards I started to work as an accompanist. But I had only one ambition: to be a repetiteur with Mahler at the opera. Fried said to me, "There's only one thing that interests Mahler, and that's his compositions." I had made a piano reduction of his Second Symphony,[1] and the following year, when I was on tour with a Dutch cellist, Jacques van Lier, we went to Vienna. I took the opportunity to call on Mahler and play the scherzo to him. I knew it and didn't need the music. He was very astonished that anyone should already know his music by heart. He seemed very pleased and I asked him for a recommendation. "That's not necessary," he said, "A recommendation can be faked. Go to Rainer Simons.[2] Tell him I sent you and it will be all right."

I went, but it was not all right. Simons just said, "Thank you for your visit. Good morning." I went back to Mahler and told him that it was absolutely essential that I should have a written recommendation. He took a visiting card and wrote on it.[3] I tell you this recommendation opened every door for me. The next day I went back to Berlin and there I had it photographed and sent copies to, I think, twelve theatres in Germany in the hope of an engagement. Mahler had

---

[1] Subsequently lost during Klemperer's years in America.

[2] Director of the Vienna Volksoper 1903–1917, 1926–1931.

[3] "Gustav Mahler recommends Herr Klemperer as an outstandingly good musician. In spite of his youth he is already experienced and is pre-destined for the career of a conductor. He (Mahler) vouches for the favourable outcome of any probationary appointment and is willing personally to provide further information."

warned me, "It's always the first engagement that is so difficult. Later on it comes of itself." But by chance that recommendation got me my first position in Prague.

At that time there was an annual meeting of an association for new music[1]— I think its founder was Liszt, and in 1907 it was to take place in Dresden. I was a member of this association and I thought, I'll go; perhaps something will turn up. After all the concerts—among other things I heard Schoenberg's First Quartet played by the Rosé Quartet—I was sitting alone at a restaurant, when I heard two men talking at a nearby table. One of them said, "We need a conductor in Prague." I would have liked to have stood up and said, "Here he is." I didn't dare, but after they had left I asked the waiter who the gentlemen were. One was a Bohemian music critic, Dr Richard Batka. I went to his hotel, but the hall porter told me he had just left. I rushed to the station. In the waiting room I found this Dr Batka and gave him Mahler's card. He said, "Go to Marienbad right away. Angelo Neumann,[2] the director of the Prague theatre, is there. Tell him I sent you."

I travelled third class throughout the night from Dresden to Marienbad. In the morning I introduced myself to Neumann, who was in bed—he was suffering badly from prostate trouble, and had to take care of himself. I had a big package of compositions under my arm, as I felt that somehow I had to introduce myself musically. These didn't interest him at all, but Mahler's introduction did a great deal. In his rather theatrical way, he said, "I herewith offer you the position that twenty years ago I offered to Nikisch. You will come to Prague in the middle of August as chorus master and conductor. What do you want to conduct?" No one had said that to me before! I said, *Carmen*, and perhaps *Rigoletto* and *Der Freischütz*. He said, "Bravo", and the conversation seemed to be at an end. I said, "Mr Neumann, I must have that in writing." "You don't need that with me," he replied. "No, no. I have been let down by other theatre directors.[3] If you don't put it in writing, I won't come." He gave me a piece of paper like a contract and the following day confirmation reached me in Berlin. I was engaged for five years at a salary that certainly wasn't high.

On August 15 I reported to the German Opera House in Prague. There the man in the office said, "What's your name, what do you want?" I told him I had

[1] Allgemeine Deutsche Musikverein.

[2] 1838–1910. Originally a singer, later impresario and theatre director. Neumann was the first man to mount *The Ring* outside Bayreuth (Leipzig 1878) and to tour the production (London 1882). In 1885 he became director of the Deutsches Landestheater (the German as opposed to Czech opera house) in Prague and in the following year he appointed Mahler conductor. Mahler remained with Neumann until 1888, and it was under his auspices that he had his first opportunity to conduct Wagner.

[3] A tactical untruth.

been engaged. "Where, here? Mr Neumann has said nothing to us." Then I took out his letter and everything was all right. *Quod non est in actis, non est in mundo.* The next day I had a chorus rehearsal for *Madame Butterfly* and fourteen days later I conducted *Der Freischütz*.

The producer told me that for a repertory performance of this sort there would only be one rehearsal, as the cast all knew their roles. I replied, "No, no. I need two rehearsals, one with the orchestra alone and one with the cast and the orchestra." I said that otherwise I wouldn't conduct. I got two rehearsals and this performance of *Der Freischütz* was for me a decisive success. One sees that one shouldn't always say "Yes".

I stayed three years in Prague. In the first year I conducted almost only operettas; *The Merry Widow* and *A Waltz Dream*—that was terribly popular at that time. Then I moved up to *Martha* and *Cavalleria Rusticana*, and, above all, Meyerbeer's *Les Huguenots*. Why isn't that performed today? The fourth act is incomparable. I got as far as *The Flying Dutchman* and *Lohengrin*. But in the spring of 1908 I was fairly ill with an inflammation of the glands. I had to be operated on and when I returned to the theatre I was still in a weak condition. Neumann took one look at me and sent me on four weeks holiday to Meran with all expenses paid. That was an act of generosity that I will not forget.

But then came disaster. Neumann was constantly attacked—and not without reason—in the Prague paper, *Bohemia*. I knew the music critic, Felix Adler. Though I didn't meet him often, we were good friends. Neumann regarded me as the instigator of these bad criticisms, and when another unfavourable review appeared, he said,

"That criticism is by you."

"By me?"

"Yes. The tone is yours. You have the choice, either you cease to meet him, or you leave my theatre."

So I gave up my position, or rather, I was given up.

I sent telegrams and wrote in all directions and found that there was a vacant position in Hamburg. Once again I turned to Mahler in my need. He sent a nice cable[1] to the Opera House and I was engaged. That was in 1910. At Hamburg I was co-conductor with Gustav Brecher—an excellent *chef*. He was particularly good with singers. But his end was terrible. He was married to a daughter of a director of AEG.[2] He was one of those Jews who refused to leave Germany after the Nazis had come to power, even after the concentration camps had been set up, because they didn't want to lose their property. But finally he and his wife lost everything. In 1940 they got to Lisbon. But their permission to travel to the

---

[1] "*Klemperer zugreifen.*" ("Seize Klemperer.")

[2] Allgemeine Elektrizitätsgesellschaft. A huge electrical concern.

United States hadn't arrived, so in early June they returned to Brussels. From there they went to Ostend, where a fisherman said he would ferry them over to England. Nothing more was ever heard of them. Terrible.

I began at Hamburg in September 1910 with *Lohengrin*. In my entire life up to today I've never had such a success as I had then. It was unbelievable. The papers wrote of a meteor. I had a wonderful cast. The first of the four boys was Elisabeth Schumann, the second was Lotte Lehmann.

And then I conducted *Rigoletto* with Caruso. He himself was charming, but his manager was terrible. He told me that when Caruso came into the theatre I would have to stop the rehearsal and do those parts in which Caruso appeared. But when he appeared and the manager tried to stop the rehearsal, Caruso said, "Let the young man finish." He was very charming and rehearsed like any other singer. Once I told him that he was dragging and he took my advice. He also sang in *Carmen* and Flotow's *Martha*, an old German opera but very effective, and I conducted these operas also.

Afterwards the director called me to say that Caruso had been very pleased with my conducting and on that account an advance that I had received would be a present. Incidentally, Caruso told me how much he had learnt from Polish Jewish cantors. Whenever he was in a town with a synagogue on Friday evening he went to hear the singing. The cantors in eastern Europe are outstanding. They generally have high baritone voices, not tenors.

Now I want to tell you something that is very important for my whole life. At first everything went well in Hamburg. But my mood became darker and darker. I was also very depressed about this regime in the theatre, every day another opera and never properly rehearsed. I was really ill. I mean psychologically ill. I could see no way out. My father saw my condition and travelled to Berlin to talk to Georg Klemperer,[1] my cousin, who was a famous doctor. My cousin said that if I would like to go away for a while, he would pay. So the most important question was solved. I left the theatre for a year and went to Strasbourg, because my old teacher, Hans Pfitzner, lived there. I stayed just outside Strasbourg, at Schiltigheim, with an Alsatian family, who spoke only French. I wanted that, so as to learn more of the language. But mainly I studied scores, especially *The Ring*, Mozart operas and, later, Strauss operas. I really studied. I mean study; that means going into the work—not just looking at it and then conducting it. That year when I was not in practical work in the theatre was the most important for my whole development.

HEYWORTH: Like a year of retreat?

KLEMPERER: Absolutely. And I must say that some of today's young conductors should do the same. They would see that one learns a lot, if one is alone.

[1] 1865–1946. Director of the Moabit Hospital in Berlin.

HEYWORTH: So you feel that these periods of depression from which you've suffered have served a fruitful function?

KLEMPERER: Oh yes. Even in depressions—I have an up and down nature, you see—I have always worked. Even in depressions. That is very important for anyone in the same condition. When you cannot work, life is finished.

About this time I first got to know Richard Strauss. It was in 1911 at a Liszt centenary festival in Heidelberg, where he was conducting Liszt's Second Piano Concerto with Busoni as soloist. Not bad! I mean, the piece may be a bit superficial, particularly at the end, but the performance was brilliant. I had met Strauss briefly in Berlin in 1906, when I had called on him with Mahler's recommendation. But at Heidelberg I got to know him better. I even played him some orchestral songs I had written. He was very impressed and said we must hear them at the next Allgemeine Deutsche Musikfest. But the work wasn't accepted, though I thought it was quite good.

As I told you, I had heard *Tod und Verklärung* as a young boy in Hamburg, and it had made a great impression on me. At that time in the nineties Strauss was the coming man for the Germans. He was sacrosanct. Later,[1] *Salome* was an immense sensation, and even today simply as sound it is an extraordinary piece. Mahler did everything he could to put it on in Vienna, though he didn't succeed. He always supported Strauss's music. And Strauss was an admirer of Mahler's music. He said that the adagio of the Fourth Symphony was a piece he could not have composed himself. They got on well, though Strauss said he was always a little afraid when he was with Mahler. Which one can understand; they were very different characters.

Strauss was present at the concert at Essen, when Mahler conducted the first performance of his Sixth Symphony. As I told you, Mahler was deeply moved by the work, which he felt to be specially personal. It so happened that the burgomaster died the same day, and after the concert Strauss came into the conductor's room and said, "Mahler, you'll have to conduct something for the burgomaster." Then he looked around, "Well, what's wrong with all you people, you look very sad and depressed." He just couldn't understand the impact of the symphony.

I first heard *Salome* under Schuch in Dresden in 1907, and two years later in Prague *Elektra* was performed there in Czech by the Czech National Theatre, not by the German Opera. That was splendid. Then came *Der Rosenkavalier* and everything was drowned in sugared water. Of the works Strauss wrote after *Der Rosenkavalier*, I find *Ariadne auf Naxos* the best, that's the last work he finished before the First World War.[2] Then he wrote *Die Frau ohne Schatten*, which I really don't understand—the text, I mean. It's strange that with the war he came to

[1] 1905.   [2] Refers to the first version of 1912.

a full stop. After all, those late works are not important, though *Metamorphosen* I find basically quite nice. I conducted it in Budapest after the last war.

HEYWORTH: What was he like as a man?

KLEMPERER: A very agreeable man. I mean, polite and conventional, but also witty. On a tour of South America with the Vienna Philharmonic he conducted a Bruckner symphony and afterwards he told members of the committee, who had put on the concert, "That's the way our peasants compose." Look, he was a great man. I know that. But, goodness, how can I explain? In *Mahagonny*[1] a character says, "Something is lacking." And in the character of Strauss something was also lacking.

He was always ready to make concessions. I don't know if you know the revisions in the text of *Der Rosenkavalier* that Herr von Hülsen made for Berlin when it was first performed there, so as to do away with some of the sexual insinuations. All that had to be removed, and Strauss agreed—after all, he got the same royalties. For him it was all one, the text. Hofmannsthal was very upset. But there was nothing he could do about it.

There was something opportunist in his character. In the summer of 1932 I was staying in Ellmau, a small place in Bavaria. My wife[2] had rehearsals for *Die Deutsche Musikbuhne*[3] and among other things she was singing the role of Christine in Strauss's *Intermezzo*. Strauss came over—Ellmau is very close to Garmisch, where he lived—and was very pleased. Then I said to him, "You know, I have to conduct *Der Rosenkavalier* and *Ein Heldenleben* next year in Berlin, and there are one or two points I would like to have your advice on. So we made a date, and later we went over to Garmisch to tea. Strauss and his wife were there, and the Jewish daughter-in-law, *née* Grab, from Prague, but not the son. First I asked him about passages in the works. He couldn't actually tell me much. "Oh, you know, I'm always glad when I'm over those passages." Well, that wasn't really much help.

Anyway, we drank tea and naturally the talk turned to the theme of the day, the Nazis, who were obviously coming to power. Strauss said, "But, tell me, what will happen to the German theatres and opera houses if the Jews leave?"[4] Frau Strauss turned to me. "Herr Doktor, if the Nazis give you any trouble, just you come to me. I'll show those gentlemen who's who." Strauss looked at her in surprise. "That would be just the right moment to stand up for a Jew!" The shame-

---

[1] *Der Aufsteig und Fall der Stadt Mahagonny* by Kurt Weill.
[2] Johanna Geissler (1888–1956). German soprano. After her marriage in 1919 for a while also sang under the name of Klee. See p. 53.
[3] A touring ensemble, maintained by the Prince of Reuss.
[4] As Dr Klemperer tells this story, both Strauss and his wife speak in a broad Bavarian dialect, impossible to reproduce in English.

lessness was so naked one couldn't be angry. I said nothing and later we left. I didn't see him again until after the war. There he sat in the best hotel in Pontresina. At that time he had no money. All his royalties were confiscated as enemy property. But Dr Roth[1] of Boosey & Hawkes sent him a monthly allowance and he was able to live comfortably in a Swiss hotel. It was as though nothing had happened.

But then the whole of Strauss's development was highly unsympathetic. I mean, that he accepted the Nazis with such unconcern.[2] Why didn't he leave? He was Richard Strauss, famous throughout the whole world, and if he had left Germany, then people would have realised that the outlook there was black. But no, he stayed. And why? Because in Germany there were fifty-six opera houses and in America only two—New York and San Francisco. He said it himself, "That would have reduced my income." At the end of his life Strauss revised everything possible, naturally to get royalties. For instance, he made a waltz suite from *Der Rosenkavalier*. Terrible. I heard it immediately before a pot-pourri from Offenbach's *La Vie Parisienne* and I found the Offenbach much, much better.

But he was someone. I mean, he had real authority—as a conductor as well as a composer.

HEYWORTH: What was he like as a conductor?

KLEMPERER: He only made very small movements, but their effect was enormous. His control of the orchestra was absolute. I especially liked his Mozart. I have an unforgettable memory of the performances he conducted at the old Residenz theatre in Munich. They were enchanting. He accompanied the recitative himself on a harpsichord, and made delightful little decorations. *Don Giovanni*, *Figaro* and *Così fan tutte* were all excellent.

HEYWORTH: Did Strauss seem to have a new approach to Mozart?

KLEMPERER: I think he had. For instance, before 1914 *Così fan tutte* was almost unknown. When I saw Busoni in Zürich in 1918, I discovered to my amazement that he didn't know the work at all. I sent him a score and he wrote that he had "lapped up the music". It was performed, but generally in terrible arrangements with other titles, and naturally in German. Strauss was the first to see its enormous value. And then about 1905 I heard his *Tristan*. Very good. And his *Meistersinger*. Excellent. That was in Berlin with Bertram, a very famous baritone at that time,

[1] Ernst Roth (1896–1971). Subsequently the chairman of Boosey & Hawkes, Strauss's publisher after the Second World War.

[2] In 1933 Strauss accepted the presidency of the *Reichsmusikkammer*, an organisation set up by the Nazis to direct musical life in Germany. He resigned in 1935. In 1933 he stood in at concerts in Leipzig, when storm-troopers prevented Walter from conducting, and at Bayreuth, when Toscanini refused to conduct there.

also with Emmy Destinn as Eva and Kraus as Walther. And an excellent orchestra. No, it was very good.

You see, the difference between a conductor like, say, Nikisch on the one hand and Strauss and Mahler on the other is that Strauss and Mahler were composers, first composers and then conductors. The creative was also evident in Strauss's conducting. When he conducted Mozart it was particularly splendid, because Strauss was also apparent in it. And the way in which Strauss conducted his own music was miraculous. For instance, under him *Elektra* sounded like an opera by Lortzing. He really understood how to let an orchestra breathe. *He* didn't throw himself around like a madman, but the orchestra played as though *it* were possessed.

HEYWORTH: Could one say that Clemens Krauss was his successor in this respect?

KLEMPERER: You could say it, but it would be untrue; fundamentally untrue. Clemens Krauss was a gifted conductor, but unimportant; quite unimportant. Strauss's successor today? I don't really know of any.

Have I told you about Strauss and Beethoven's Fifth Symphony? In the summer of 1928 he and I were both staying at the Waldhaus Hotel in Sils Maria and we sometimes went for walks. On one of these occasions he said to me, "You know, I can't conduct a Beethoven symphony unless I have some sort of picture before me." "Really," I said, "and what sort of picture?" "Well now, for instance, the second movement of the Fifth is the farewell from the beloved, and when the trumpets enter that is onward to higher goals." Isn't that incredible? I couldn't believe my ears.

HEYWORTH: But he conducted Beethoven well none the less?

KLEMPERER: No. The Fifth Symphony was not good. But, all in all, he was, of course, a wonderful conductor.

In 1911 I returned to Hamburg. But then the following year I fell into the other extreme of a euphoria of unequalled intensity, and owing to a purely personal matter I had to leave. Finally, in 1913, I got another engagement at Barmen as first conductor. Although it was really an awful step down, I learnt an immense amount there. As musical director I was really able to get to grips with the whole material of an operatic theatre. I produced *Così fan tutte* as well as conducting it. I conducted *The Ring* for the first time, and on January 4, 1914, I conducted *Parsifal*, which was one of the first performances given outside Bayreuth, after the work had been freed on January 1, 1914. Then later that year I went to Strasbourg at the request of Pfitzner, who was musical director there.

HEYWORTH: How had you come into contact with Pfitzner?

KLEMPERER: Pfitzner was professor of composition when I went to the Stern Conservatory in Berlin. That was in 1904. I joined his class right away and I showed him everything I wrote. I always had the feeling that he didn't really like giving lessons. He wanted to write his own music, but he didn't earn enough from it.

But one could learn from him. He also had a class in conducting. One of the students had to play the piano, another conducted—and Pfitzner sang! We went through *Tristan* and *Götterdämmerung* in this way. It was very useful. I mean, I learnt the works.

Later, I don't know exactly when,[1] Pfitzner became director of the opera as well as of the conservatory in Strasbourg. In 1914, he sent a friend to Barmen to ask me if I would take over the opera for a year, as he wanted to orchestrate *Palestrina*. I warned his friend that it wasn't a good idea, that two parties would form in Strasbourg, one for Pfitzner and one for me. You see, Pfitzner was no great conductor. He was a very fine musician, but he wasn't a conductor. His emissary said, "What, you as competition to Pfitzner!" So I went to Strasbourg and there it finally came to very disagreeable words.

My first opera was *Fidelio*. Pfitzner was accustomed to cut the whole beginning of the last scene up to the first words of the Minister, "Des bestens Königs Wink und Wille". He found the opening chorus too foursquare. Ridiculous! Naturally, I restored the cut. Pfitzner made awful trouble. He told me that I was only his deputy, that I must do as he did. "You have to give my version," he said. I replied, "I'm giving Beethoven's version."

The following year was worse still, as Pfitzner took up his post again as opera director. I retained my position as deputy director, but I had to conduct second-rate things. He gave *Fidelio* to Fried[2] and I was beside myself. I determined not to conduct any work that he produced—we had quite different conceptions of the scenic realisation of an opera—and as a result I refused to conduct Marschner's *Hans Heiling*. Our relationship grew worse from month to month. Together with a captain in the army, Pfitzner and his wife summoned me before an almost formal tribunal at the conservatory and accused me of bribing critics, so that he got bad notices and I got good ones! Naturally, there wasn't a word of truth in it. The whole season was fruitless for me, though I must say that I very much liked a *Zauberflöte* that he both conducted and produced. Then the situation grew easier, as in 1916 Pfitzner resigned as opera director, so that during my last season in Strasbourg I had complete freedom of decision.

HEYWORTH: Then you went to Cologne?

KLEMPERER: Yes. After a successful guest appearance in *Fidelio* I was engaged in 1917. But before I left Strasbourg we had to find a new conductor. It so happened that that year I went to Zürich to hear Strauss conduct his new version of *Ariadne*.[3] I

---

[1] 1910.

[2] Oscar Fried's brother.

[3] *Ariadne auf Naxos*. The second version with the newly composed prologue, which is generally performed today, had had its first performance in Vienna in 1916.

talked to Strauss, and he said, "Take Szell.[1] He's playing the piano tonight in *Ariadne* and he's extremely talented." I met Szell and he was very charming and witty and bright. But too young; I think he was only nineteen. We wanted to engage him at Strasbourg, so we said he was twenty-two. He came as a guest and conducted *Carmen* and *Ariadne*, both very well. Later in Berlin[2] he often came to my rehearsals. But after the last war we didn't see much of each other. He was a very good conductor, but ice-cold.

The orchestra at Cologne was splendid. But otherwise it was a real repertory theatre: every day a different opera, all badly rehearsed. I began with *Figaro* in September 1917. The director of the theatre, Hofrat Fritz Remond—a former Wagner tenor—produced and it was terrible. For the first time I felt how unjust I had been to reject Pfitzner's productions. The whole season was disagreeable, because Remond always produced, and the power he had was the reason why I eventually left seven years later.

But in my second season I was able to establish opera house concerts and I also got the right to produce some operas. The standard of the Cologne opera wasn't high, though when I compare it with the standard of most German opera houses today, it was very good. Friedrich Schorr was in the company and one of my conductors was Paul Dessau. He had shown me some of his early compositions. I found them good and when a position became free I took him. He was my repetiteur for many years. Another was Hans Wilhelm Steinberg,[3] who is today a well-known conductor.

It was in Cologne that I became *Generalmusikdirektor*. A new cellist was needed by the orchestra, and many instrumentalists came for auditions to Herr Abendroth, the conductor of the Gürzenich Concerts[4] and *meine Wenigkeit*.[5] But we couldn't agree: I preferred X and he preferred Y. It ended with our both going to the Lord Mayor, Adenauer,[6] who certainly had more important things to do than to worry about the engagement of a cellist. Abendroth began, "If Herr Klemperer's proposal is accepted, my position is impossible and I resign." Thereupon Adenauer turned to me: "Now we don't want Herr Abendroth to resign, do we?" I really should have said, "Yes, I do." But I answered, "Naturally not." "Well then, let us agree to his proposal." The Oberbürgermeister said good-bye, but then added, "Herr Klemperer, I'd like to speak to you alone for a moment." Abendroth disappeared and then Adenauer said, "I only wanted to tell you that the city

---

[1] George Szell (1897–1970). Conductor of the Cleveland Orchestra 1946–1970.
[2] Szell was a conductor at the Staatsoper 1924–1929.
[3] Today better known as William Steinberg. Conductor of the Boston Orchestra 1970–2.
[4] Series of concerts by the opera orchestra given in the Gürzenich Hall.
[5] Literally, "my small self".
[6] Konrad Adenauer (1876–1967). First Chancellor of the Federal German Republic 1949–1964.

has decided to grant you the title and the function of *Generalmusikdirektor*."[1]

In my second year in Cologne Universal Edition sent me a score of Janáček's *Jenůfa*. It really made an excellent impression on me. I recommended it to the Intendant[2] and it was decided to perform it. We had started rehearsals, when suddenly the chorus declared that it refused to give an opera by a composer whose fellow-countrymen were ruining German lands and raping German women.[3] Thank God nothing came of this protest and on 16 November, 1918 we gave the work its first German performance with great success. Later I gave the first German performance of *Katya Kabanová*;[4] and also of the Sinfonietta. But that was later in Berlin.[5]

HEYWORTH: While you were in Cologne, you gave the first performance of Schreker's[6] *Irrelohe*.[7] I imagine that he then seemed a more important figure than he does now?

KLEMPERER: Schreker played a great role in German musical life at that time, and I also conducted *Der ferne Klang* and *Schatzgräber*. At that period he seemed a revolutionary. When Dr Rottenberg conducted the first performance of *Der ferne Klang* in Frankfurt in 1912, he called for Schreker because they didn't know what to make of the score. In fact, one act *is* very complicated. That was his first opera and it was an enormous success. Paul Bekker, the critic of the *Frankfurter Zeitung*, wrote that there had been nothing like it since Richard Wagner. Later he claimed that the love duet in *Der Schatzgräber* was the best since *Tristan*.

Then came opera after opera. Schreker was very much *en vogue*. The operas all had an erotic background, but very effectively handled, so that theatres fought for the right to give the premières. I think that for a few years his operas were even more performed than Strauss's. But then came the decline. *Irrelohe* still went fairly well, though Weissmann from the *BZ*[8]—a critic who was much feared—attacked it savagely. Schreker was very unhappy, but that didn't stop him from asking me if I wouldn't like to do another of his operas. "Quite by chance, I have a review from Elberfeld,"[9] he said, and showed it as evidence of what a wonderful work it was!

Then finally came that terrible session of the Prussian Academy of the Arts

[1] In Germany *Generalmusikdirektor*, like Professor, is a title that is bestowed as well as a position.
[2] Administrative head of the opera house.
[3] Janáček was a Czech and in the final stages of the First World War Bohemia had revolted against Austrian rule.
[4] The first performance outside Czechoslovakia.
[5] 1927, at the opening concert of the Kroll Opera. See p. 59.
[6] Franz Schreker (1878–1934). Austrian composer.
[7] 1924.
[8] *BZ am Mittag*. A large Berlin paper.
[9] A small town in the Ruhr.

in 1933, in which Schillings,[1] who was president, got up and said that the Führer wanted to break the Jewish influence on German music. Whereupon Schoenberg picked up his hat and said, "You don't need to say that to me twice," and left. But not Schreker, who was director of the Hochschule für Musik;[2] he stubbornly insisted that he wasn't a Jew. Of course it finally came out that he was. He had to go, and after that not a note of his music was heard. The success of his operas disappeared overnight. The strange thing is that Schreker and Schoenberg were close friends.[3] Schoenberg rarely went out, but he always attended performances of Schreker's operas.

HEYWORTH: Do you think Schreker tried to be the German Puccini?

KLEMPERER: Surely. Ho, ho, how much he would have liked to have been! But the melodic talent wasn't there. It was typical inflation music.[4]

We did Pfitzner's *Palestrina* in Cologne and Pfitzner himself spent weeks and weeks producing it. He was certainly talented, but I think he was a better writer than a composer. The text of *Palestrina* is wonderful; there are passages that one could compare with Goethe. The music I don't find so important, though it's good, in part even effective. And I find the music of a fairy tale, *Das Christelflein*, charming; it has a really enchanting overture. When Pfitzner came to Cologne we were friends again, because I was doing *Palestrina*. But by then our tastes were so different that I could not always go along with him musically.

HEYWORTH: When you first knew him was he already against "modern" tendencies in music?

KLEMPERER: Not at the time I first knew him. But later he wrote violent attacks on Busoni[5] and Paul Bekker.

HEYWORTH: His book, *Die neue Aesthetik der musikalischen Impotenz* ends with a violent assault on the Jews for their destructive influence on music. Who did he have in mind?

KLEMPERER: Mahler, Schoenberg, Schreker. Earlier he had written in an article, "What does one do if the *creator spiritus* doesn't come?" Of course he meant Mahler, who had composed "Veni creator spiritus" in his Eighth Symphony.

[1] Max von Schillings (1868–1933). German conductor and composer. Intendant of the Berlin State Opera 1918–1925. See page 56.

[2] Leading state conservatory in Berlin.

[3] Both men were Viennese and separated by only four years in age. Schreker, who conducted the first performance of *Gurrelieder* in Vienna in 1913, was an early supporter of Schoenberg's music—something that Schoenberg, who was fiercely loyal, never forgot. Further evidence of the close relations between the two men is provided by the fact that Alban Berg, who was then still virtually a pupil of Schoenberg, made the piano reduction of *Der ferne Klang*.

[4] A reference to the acute inflation that Germany suffered in early twenties, when Schreker's fame was at its height.

[5] Pfitzner strongly disapproved of the neo-classicism heralded by Busoni.

a Gustav Mahler's letter to Ferdinand Gregori, *Intendant* of the Mannheim Opera, 1910

b Silhouette, Strasbourg, about 1916

c Drawing by Otto Dix, 1923

d Woodcut by Ewald Dülberg, 1917

e Woodcut by Ernst-Ludwig Kirchner, 1915–16

Hochverehrter Herr!
Mit Freuden empfehle ich Herrn Klemperer, dem ich alle Eigenschaften zuschreibe, die einen Kapellmeister grossen Styles ausmachen. Er ist allerdings noch sehr jung, aber er hat Zukunft, und ich bin überzeugt, dass Sie gar keine bessere Wal (Wahl) treffen können.

Hochachtungsvoll ergeben,
Gustav Mahler

Dear Sir,
It is with pleasure that I recommend Herr Klemperer, to whom I attribute all the qualities of a conductor of great stature. He is admittedly still very young. But he has a future and I am convinced that you could not make a better choice.

Yours truly,
Gustav Mahler

a Arriving for the first time in New York with his wife, 1926

b Walking in the Swiss mountains about 1926

c With his wife in Westerland on the isle of Sylt about 1930

d With his children, Werner and Lotte, in Berlin about 1931

Whereupon Bekker wrote that Pfitzner should say whom he meant; surely he didn't mean Mahler, to whom he owed so much. For Mahler had been the first to perform *Die Rose vom Liebesgarten* in a major theatre, in Vienna. He was enchanted by the work. Not only that, he told Pfitzner to sit directly behind him during rehearsals and to interrupt when anything didn't please him. "I would really like to hear your critical opinion," he said. "I criticise the orchestra so often that they should know that I also can take criticism." The production was a great success and it was often performed.

But Pfitzner not only esteemed Mahler, he loved him. I will not be silent about this. He always said that Mahler was full of humanity and a great man. Only with his music he was not *d'accord*. Schoenberg's music Pfitzner hardly knew. I don't think he really understood it, just as Strauss, when he saw the score of Schoenberg's *Five Pieces for Orchestra*, said, "I can't discuss it seriously. It's nonsense." He considered it not just musically puzzling, but sick and pathological. Goodness, if only he had known what has come since!

Pfitzner was no philo-Semite. But he wasn't anti-Semitic either. He liked Jews who he considered to be good Germans and he hated any sort of internationalism. For instance, I had a little party for him after the war, when he was producing *Palestrina* in Cologne, and to make it more interesting I invited Max Scheler,[1] the philosopher. After dinner Scheler had the unhappy idea of reading aloud a poem by Claudel—in French, naturally. As he began, Pfitzner got up and left. I went after him and asked him why. "I cannot stand someone reading a French poem in these times." That was his position. A little crazy.

Later on[2] he had a composition class at the Music Academy in Munich. But I don't think he had many pupils. I think he hoped that the National Socialists would give him his hour of glory. But even in the Nazi period he didn't have great success. They regarded him as a good composer, but they didn't like his difficult personality. Naturally, he was angry about this. And then in the last war English bombs destroyed his house in Munich. After the war his situation was really very difficult. His wife had died years before and he had to live in an old people's home.

HEYWORTH: Did you see him after the war?

KLEMPERER: I saw him in this home outside Munich and asked him whether I could help him in any way or whether he needed money. He said, "No. The best thing you could do would be to put on a performance of *Das Herz*."[3] That was written after *Palestrina*. It's a very bad piece. He complained about this and that. He

---

[1] 1874–1928. Well known German philosopher, who applied Husserl's phenomenology to the field of ethics and religion. A forerunner of Heidegger.

[2] 1930–1934.

[3] First performed 1931.

D

had to be de-Nazified. That didn't please him and it *was* a bit crazy; I mean, why did this world have to occupy itself with Pfitzner, a composer who was hardly known outside Germany. But he could also be very witty—that was his best quality. When his house was bombed, for instance, he said, "Look, and they say that *mir nichts einfällt*."[1] Very good.

But he also did unpleasant things. I don't know if the name Paul Nikolaus Cossmann means anything to you. He was editor of the *Süddeutsche Monatshefte*, which was in favour of Bavarian separatism: Bavaria shouldn't be part of Germany, but should have close ties with Austria. That was not a line that appealed to Hitler, and Cossmann, who was a Jew though a baptised Catholic, was immediately put into a concentration camp and died there. Bruno Walter, who knew Pfitzner well, wrote to him after the war and asked what had happened to Cossmann. Whereupon Pfitzner answered, "Cossmann died peacefully in a concentration camp." That was less than sympathetic. I mean, how "peacefully" he died in a concentration camp is more than questionable.

The Vienna Philharmonic Orchestra behaved very well to Pfitzner after the war. They arranged a house for him in Salzburg, where he could live quietly, and, in return he gave them the manuscript of *Palestrina*. He died in Salzburg in 1949, just a few months before Strauss.

HEYWORTH: Would it be true to say that your intellectual horizons began to expand during your Strasbourg years?

KLEMPERER: Yes. Shortly after I arrived there, the war broke out and the theatre was shut. The company was told that it would perhaps reopen on January 1, 1915 (as it did). In the meantime married personnel were paid 200 marks, unmarried 150. I got 150 marks; it wasn't much, but it was enough. I spent those months in Munich and it was there that I first got to know the works of Schopenhauer, which of course made an immense impression on me, even if there is much in them that I didn't understand, because, basically, I'm uneducated—at any rate in philosophical matters. As I told you, I didn't even take my *Abitur*, and don't know any Greek, and that makes everything very hard. In Strasbourg I read Spinoza's *Ethics* and found them wonderful. Later I came to Nietzsche. I found him marvellous and not only because Mahler set a few words of his in his Third Symphony. And his battle against Wagner seemed to me both important and right.

HEYWORTH: Do you still find it justified?

KLEMPERER: Yes. He showed that one shouldn't take Wagner's tragic pretensions all that seriously. When he began *The Ring*, Wagner based it on the figure of Siegfried, a hero, who brings a new order, didn't he? That was something he took

---

[1] A pun. *Einfallen*, literally, to fall in (i.e. the roof has fallen in), also means to have an idea.

from Feuerbach,[1] whom he was friendly with. Then he discovered Schopenhauer's writings and thereupon he suddenly changed. Schopenhauer's thought leads to nihilism: everything falls apart, and Nietzsche was the first to point out this discrepancy in *The Ring*. He was also the first to say that Wagner was above all else an actor, that he understood only too well the art of theatrical effectiveness.

Yet I must confess that when I recently[2] conducted the first act of *Die Walküre* it was as though I were encountering a woman I had loved forty years ago. And the strange thing was that she hadn't changed or grown older. I find the music thrilling. Thrilling! One can say this or that about Wagner, but no one else could have written that music. No one! It's as stupid to underestimate Wagner as it is to overestimate him. He doesn't need either.

HEYWORTH: But what do you call overestimate? I mean, if I said that Wagner was the greatest dramatist since Shakespeare, would you call that overestimating him?

KLEMPERER: Considerably overestimating him. (Laughter.) And if you say Wagner was a poet like Goethe, I would say: *Schweinerei*. Wagner's operas are the development of works by Weber and Marschner, the first romantics, aren't they? I would even say a magnificent development, a point of culmination. But they led to a dead end. You can't continue on that road better or further than he did. I mean, everything that appears today, for instance Beckett's plays, which I find wonderful, comes from total opposition to Wagner. What I find so offensive is when he virtually describes himself as Beethoven's successor. That he really is not. I mean, Beethoven was in the first place a composer of symphonies. That he also wrote an opera, a fine one, is not the point. But Wagner wrote no symphonies and no chamber music.

HEYWORTH: But can one not say that there is a symphonic element, even if not in the precise meaning of the word, in his later operas, without which he could not have sustained the dimensions of *The Ring*?

KLEMPERER: Yes, of course. That one can say. That is also true.

But to return to my Strasbourg years. Much of the intellectual stimulus in my life at that time was due to Georg Simmel.[3] He had come to Strasbourg as *ordentlicher*[4] professor of philosophy immediately before the war. He came from Berlin, where it was impossible for him to become *Ordinarius* on racial grounds.

[1] Ludwig Feuerbach (1804–72). German philosopher who marks a transition between Hegelian dialectic and bourgeois (i.e. non-Marxist) materialism. His political optimism is reflected in the early drafts of *The Ring*.

[2] 1969.

[3] 1858–1918. Philosopher and sociologist.

[4] An *Ordinarius*, or head of a faculty, as opposed to a common or garden professor, a breed that proliferates in Central Europe, thus compelling a further grade in a society addicted to hierarchical distinctions.

I not only attended his lectures, but often visited him, when we talked about many things. He was very kind to me. He said, we don't need only to discuss "important" matters; we can just talk. He was very much interested in music and especially late Beethoven. Mozart he didn't understand so well. But then I invited him to a performance of *Don Giovanni*, and when I saw him afterwards he said, "You are right. There is something daemonic in Mozart that I didn't see before tonight."

That was about the time I was beginning to read Spinoza's *Ethics* and I talked to Simmel about it. He told me, "Just read the propositions, not the proofs, for they are not made better by the proofs. If you read the propositions carefully, then you will know what you need to know." A great man.

It was interesting to see the reaction of a supposedly free mind like Simmel's to the war. He was very nationalist and, like so many people in Germany, believed absolutely in the war and in victory. He even wrote an article in the *Frankfurter Zeitung*—"Eine Fastenpredigt"[1]—urging people to eat only what they got on their ration cards.

But during the first part of the war I was also strongly *deutschnational*[2] and I believed firmly in the victory of German arms. Then in 1918 I managed to visit Switzerland and in Zürich I talked to Busoni. He said, "If you stayed a few weeks in Switzerland, you would think differently." He was right. Defeat grew ever nearer, the so-called German Revolution began, the Kaiser went and all Germany's potentates resigned—to me an extremely welcome event. I became more or less a socialist, until I saw that that was also the wrong way for me.

In summer 1916, when I was on holiday in Königstein outside Frankfurt, Simmel sent me a manuscript. Its title was *Vom Geist der Utopie*. Only a manuscript; it wasn't printed. I wrote back that I was really too tired to study and without study I couldn't understand it. Simmel replied that I should at least read the chapters on music. I did so and found them very good. The book was printed and so I was, so to speak, in at the beginning of Ernst Bloch's[3] great career. At that time I didn't know him. I got to know him later in the twenties in Berlin, where he was then living without a university appointment. As an illustration of his way of thinking, he wrote a phrase about the *Fidelio* performance, which I conducted at the opening of the Kroll Opera and was terribly attacked. "Nirgends brennen wir genauer." A good phrase isn't it? I mean, not only to burn but to do so exactly and precisely. "Nirgends brennen wir genauer"; that made a great impression on me. I saw a lot of Bloch in Berlin. Today he's my oldest living friend. He's very musical and plays the piano very well. He's an extraordinary man.

[1] Literally, a "fasting sermon".   [2] Right-wing and patriotic.
[3] 1885– . The leading Marxist philosopher of his generation in Germany.

HEYWORTH: He has written about music, hasn't he?

KLEMPERER: Oh yes, a lot. He has written essays on Wagner and Mozart, especially on Mozart, about *Die Zauberflöte* and *Don Giovanni*. And there's an essay on Weill's *Dreigroschenoper*. Recently he published *Atheism im Christentum*—at the age of 84. An astonishing achievement. Bloch is, of course, absolutely a Marxist.

HEYWORTH: Do you consider yourself a Marxist?

KLEMPERER: No, not at all. I mean, I have sympathy with communist ideas, but not with the culture today represented by Mr Brezhnev. But I'm not a politician, only a musician. If I had a chance to take another profession, I would take history, not politics.

Another important intellectual influence on me was Max Scheler, whom I met in Cologne. He was married to Furtwängler's sister. After the First World War Cologne was the first university to have a faculty of catholic sociology and Scheler had the chair. He was much loved and much hated. The ecclesiastical party was very happy at last to have a modern philosopher, who wasn't a reactionary, on the Catholic side. But their pleasure didn't last for long. Scheler changed his views and also got divorced, so that he found himself outside the Church.

HEYWORTH: Did these philosophical interests culminate in your conversion to Catholicism?

KLEMPERER: That's a long story. Scheler had a strong influence on me, but one shouldn't suppose that I became a Catholic through him. We never discussed the matter.

When I moved from Prague to Hamburg, in 1910, I visited my cousin, Georg Klemperer, in Berlin. To my surprise, he said, now that you are beginning your German career, naturally you will be baptised. I was astonished—I had never expected that from him. I told him that I couldn't do it. Then I went home and my father said, "Oh, Georg has no idea of Judaism." But I couldn't forget what he had said. So I decided to leave the Jewish community in Hamburg and become a dissident. Later, in Strasbourg, I was very impressed by the Minster and its services. I was impressed by the music and the colours, by the whole theatre of the Catholic liturgy; and also by the discipline. I thought, my goodness, people like Mozart, Beethoven and Schubert were Catholics, it can't be all that bad. And I had had very little connection with Judaism; for instance I didn't refuse to conduct on Saturdays. So, one day, I went to a famous Catholic historian in Strasbourg. But he was not very interested in my ideas. We talked a lot and then I asked, "But, as a Catholic, do you think Goethe was a sinner?" "Naturally," he replied. So I said good-bye.

Then I went to Cologne, which is far more Catholic than Strasbourg. There I found someone who seemed the right life-companion and in 1919 we married. Her name was Johanna Geissler and she was a leading soprano at the opera; she did soubrette roles like Mignon and Ännchen in *Der Freischütz*. Her coloratura was very easy and she even sang the Queen of the Night in *Die Zauberflöte*. Well, for a Catholic marriage is a sacrament. I mean, it is not merely a matter of writing your name in a book. So I went every evening to a Jesuit priest for instruction.

HEYWORTH: Was your future wife Catholic then?

KLEMPERER: No, she was Protestant and then she changed . . . for me.

HEYWORTH: So you didn't become a Catholic to marry her?

KLEMPERER: Oh no, no, not at all. We had two children—my son Werner, who is an actor in America, and my daughter, Lotte, who is here.

HEYWORTH: But the motive behind your conversion was faith and intellectual conviction?

KLEMPERER: (after a long pause) Yes.

HEYWORTH: Though you are no longer a Catholic?

KLEMPERER: I left the Church officially in February 1967. All in all, I think that religious conviction is an entirely personal matter.

CHAPTER IV

Stravinsky, Hindemith and the Kroll Opera

IN 1918, BERLIN had two opera houses. On Unter den Linden, the capital's main street, was the State Opera (Staatsoper), frequently referred to as the Linden Opera. Far to the west, in Charlottenburg, was the Deutsches Opernhaus. In 1925, after the incorporation of Charlottenburg into Greater Berlin, this was reopened as the Municipal Opera (Städtische Oper), and with Heinz Tietjen as Intendant and Bruno Walter as musical director rapidly established itself as a rival to the State Opera.

Until 1918 the State Opera had been a court institution, run by an Intendant who was a court official. After the collapse of the Hohenzollern monarchy in 1918 control passed to the Prussian Ministry of Culture. The ministry was, however, eager to set up a second state opera that would be more representative of the newly founded Weimar Republic. It would specialise in new and unfamiliar works and new ways of doing better known works. This plan finally came to fruition in 1927, when the Staatsoper am Platz der Republik was set up with Klemperer as its director. It occupied the Kroll Theatre; hence the name by which it is usually known.

★   ★   ★

HEYWORTH: How did you come to be director of the Kroll Opera?

KLEMPERER: I must go back a few years. In 1923 Leo Blech left the Berlin State Opera on Unter den Linden to go to the Deutsches Opernhaus in Charlottenburg, and I was asked by Ministerialdirektor Kestenberg[1] on behalf of Dr Becker[2] to go to

[1] Leo Kestenberg (1882–1962). Pianist and pupil of Busoni. From 1918 until 1932 an official in the Prussian Ministry of Culture, where he played a crucial role in the reform of school music and the plan to establish a separate branch of the Berlin State Opera in the Kroll Theatre.

[2] Carl Heinrich Becker (1876–1933). Secretary of State and subsequently (1925–1930) Minister of Culture, in which positions he made an outstanding contribution to the cultural life of the Weimar Republic.

Berlin to discuss the possibility of my taking over Blech's position at the State Opera. I had long conversations with Kestenberg and Becker. I was not only to have a leading position at the State Opera, but I was to take over the opera concerts.

But I couldn't reach any understanding with Schillings, who was still Intendant. He was used to conductors having no influence on the stage, and I wanted to have that. I didn't necessarily want to produce myself, but I wanted to have a voice in the productions I conducted. I wasn't sure that I would have an independent position as long as Schillings was Intendant. I told Dr Becker this. I said I wouldn't come as long as Schillings was there. But at the same time I wasn't willing to let him use me as a weapon against Schillings. A lot of people were against him, including Dr Becker himself. I said to him, "You would like to be rid of Schillings. You want to break your marriage with him, and I should be the marriage-breaker. I don't like that." So I refused.

But there was a deeper reason. I didn't feel mature enough for Berlin. It seemed to me too quick. So they took Kleiber, who was conductor at Mannheim.

By then I had broken with Cologne. But I heard that a conductor was needed at Wiesbaden, where the Intendant was Dr Hagemann. He came to Cologne and we made a contract, which only bound me for six months and for the rest of the year I was free to do as I wanted. Naturally, the theatre at Wiesbaden was smaller than in Cologne—it was a *diminuendo* in my career rather than a *crescendo*. But in all my life I have never felt so happy as during those three years in Wiesbaden— 1924 to 1927. Hagemann was a very fine man. He met all my wishes and I was able to take part in productions. I told him that there was an excellent stage designer in Kassel, Ewald Dülberg.[1] Hagemann at once engaged him and we did *Fidelio* and *Don Giovanni* together. I also did one of the first performances of Hindemith's *Cardillac*[2] there.

For the first time in my life I was free to travel and accept engagements abroad. In 1924 I went to Russia and I continued to go there for six weeks every year until 1936. I was so impressed by the atmosphere that at one time I seriously considered moving there with my family. It turned out otherwise and it is good that it did. Later that terrible Stalinism took over.

HEYWORTH: What was the musical atmosphere like?

KLEMPERER: At that time it was absolutely free. I gave *Das Lied von der Erde* in Russian. I did the *Missa Solemnis* and even parts of *Parsifal*. The public impressed me enormously. You know, the Russians listen with their hearts, not their ears. I remember that at my first concert in Leningrad I conducted Brahms's Fourth Symphony. It's a marvellous piece, but not a work that especially excites applause.

[1] 1888–1933. 1912–15 at the Hamburg Opera, where Klemperer had met him.
[2] It had had its first performance only some weeks earlier in 1926 at Dresden under Fritz Busch.

But after that performance the entire public rose to its feet and came forward to the podium. The applause lasted a quarter of an hour; I've never experienced anything like it. Trotsky came to one of my concerts. I met him after a performance of Beethoven's Ninth Symphony. He thought that my conducting reflected German expressionism. There was nothing I could say to that! He added that it had disturbed him that one member of the chorus had got to his place late during the performance. "Yes," I said, "There's a lack of discipline in Russian orchestras and choruses." Trotsky replied, "You will never get discipline in Russia. I haven't succeeded either."

HEYWORTH: Did you also conduct opera?

KLEMPERER: I did *Carmen* at the Bolshoi in 1924 and for eight days I had the whole theatre to myself to do as I wanted. I redid a lot of the production. For instance, in the first act there was too much business that I found awful—a gypsy fiddler, a Jewish pedlar and so on, all with the intention of livening up the stage. I said, we must get rid of all that, and the chorus was furious because, as a result, a lot of them lost their fee for the evening's appearance. The orchestra was splendid, the singers were excellent and the public's enthusiasm was immense.

HEYWORTH: Was the influence of producers like Meyerhold[1] apparent in the opera?

KLEMPERER: The performances I saw at the Bolshoi were quite untouched by his influence.

HEYWORTH: And the orchestras?

KLEMPERER: Quite good. The Leningrad Philharmonic was the best. But I also heard the Persimfans Orchestra, which played without a conductor—the leader gave the necessary cues and the players sat around him, some with their backs to the audience.

In 1926 Kestenberg came to Wiesbaden.[2] He heard *Don Giovanni* and, I think, *Elektra* and he liked them. Afterwards, and without any idea of an appointment, he told me of the ministry's plan to set up an independent branch of the State Opera in the Kroll Theatre. I said, "Give me the Kroll and we'll see what I can do with it." Kestenberg was enthusiastic, but he warned me that there were difficulties. He told me that in a few weeks' time Tietjen, the new Generalintendant of the Prussian state theatres,[3] would be coming to Mainz[4] and that he would arrange for me to see him. Tietjen came and described the new position to me as a lost Elysium—ten year contract, pension, a car (I would have a car!)—and I was

[1] Vsevolod Meyerhold (1874–1939). Famous Russian producer, who worked closely with Mayakovsky. His anti-illusionism brought about a (temporary) rejuvenation of Soviet Theatre.
[2] Wiesbaden was one of a handful of provincial theatres that were controlled by the Prussian Ministry of Culture.
[3] Tietjen had been appointed to this position in addition to that which he held at the Städtische Oper.
[4] Immediately across the Rhine from Wiesbaden.

enchanted. It was practically all untrue. In September 1926 I came to Berlin, where I saw Tietjen and Kestenberg, and first of all a five year contract was proposed. I insisted on ten years, although in fact it turned out considerably shorter, didn't it?

We also discussed who I should have as assistant conductors. My choice was Zemlinsky,[1] who at that time was at the Deutsches Landestheater in Prague, and also Zweig, who was at the Deutsches Opernhaus in Charlottenburg and wanted very much to come to me. Tietjen was very satisfied with my choice. Producers were more difficult. I wanted to do some productions myself, but naturally I couldn't do them all. Eventually I took a man called Schulz-Dornburg, whom I thought would be all right. And Dülberg came as designer—there's a picture by him over there; he was both a painter and an architect. And also Curjel; I thought he would be valuable, and so he proved.

Before I left I talked to Kestenberg. He said that if difficulties should arise, he would send me a telegram, "*es geht nicht*". Later in Berlin he told me that he had had the telegram on his desk and had decided at one moment to send it and then decided not to . . .

HEYWORTH: What was the trouble?

KLEMPERER: I will tell you. We had no money, no money at all. You see the State Opera had a single budget, and the Kroll Opera, which was part of the State Opera, was included in it. We had no budget of our own, so that we had to make do with very little. Rehearsals started in the middle of August 1927. To begin with there was no rehearsal stage—and one had to be improvised in Schloss Bellevue.[2] That wasn't the only difficulty. The theatre on Unter den Linden was being reconstructed and still wasn't finished.[3] Meanwhile, its company was performing at the Kroll. We should have opened on September 1, but it was the middle of November before we could give a performance. I didn't mind that; it gave me time to prepare my operas in peace. But even then we had to share the theatre. We had it on Monday, Wednesday and Saturday, and the Linden company had it on the other days. It was terrible.

HEYWORTH: What was your basic conception when you took over the Kroll?

KLEMPERER: To make good theatre. Not avant-garde theatre, but good theatre. In all the theatres in which I had worked from 1909 to 1927, in Prague, in Hamburg, in Strasbourg, in Cologne, I had suffered from the dirt of the repertory system. Far, far too many operas were performed, they were almost all badly

[1] Alexander von Zemlinsky (1872–1942). Austrian conductor and composer. Schoenberg's brother-in-law and earlier a colleague of Klemperer's in Prague.
[2] Across the Tiergarten from the Kroll Theatre, which was opposite the Reichstag. The Kroll Theatre was destroyed during the war.
[3] Reconstruction, which should have been completed by September 1927, was not finished until May 1928.

rehearsed, or not at all, and the general *niveau* was miserable. Not *all* the performances, naturally; on a few evenings in the year, when there were new productions, they were well prepared and something was achieved. But the following evening there would be another opera—and, almost always, badly performed. That, in my opinion, is the main reason why Mahler finally left the Vienna Opera; he saw that it just wasn't possible to offer a good performance of a different opera every evening. And so unfortunately he gave up the whole thing.

At the Kroll we were in the fortunate position of only having to give a limited number of operas. We were also lucky, because most of the works we wanted to do weren't performed at the Linden Opera. The Berlin Volksbühne[1] bought many, many seats, before it even knew what was going to be performed. So that each year we only had to offer, at the most, seven to ten operas, which were then repeated very often. What I wanted to achieve at the Kroll was a good opera house that would be untouched by the bad practices of the repertory system and illuminated by the light of a new direction.

HEYWORTH: An experimental opera?

KLEMPERER: No, though sometimes it naturally came close to that. Naturally, a lot of things were done that I didn't want, though I had to admit that it was basically right to do them. For instance, to the horror of the generally conservative public I performed a suite[2] from Weill's *Dreigroschenoper* at one of our concerts, where it didn't really belong.

HEYWORTH: You say that you didn't want to make an avant-garde opera. But isn't it true that to some extent you did so, firstly in the matter of repertory, secondly in the matter of style?

KLEMPERER: Up to a point you're right, of course. I don't know how I should express it. I wanted . . . I didn't want an avant-garde opera in the sense that that term is used today. That was exactly what I didn't want. I wanted to make good theatre—just that and nothing else.

We actually opened in November with a concert, at which Schnabel played Mozart's D minor concerto and I conducted the first performance in Berlin of Janáček's *Sinfonietta*. Janáček himself was present. And then in the middle of the month came *Fidelio*.[3] I told you that I have never had such success as I had with *Lohengrin* in Hamburg. I can say that I've never had such a failure as with that *Fidelio*. The public was enthusiastic, but not the critics. One of them described it as *Fidelio* on ice. Alfred Einstein, whom I liked very much, he also could not accept it. He wrote that it was a performance without spiritual grace, without inspiration.

[1] An association that offers cheap seats on subscription to its members.
[2] In fact composed at Klemperer's instigation.
[3] Produced and conducted by Klemperer.

HEYWORTH: Why did the critics so dislike it?

KLEMPERER: Because the scenery was stylised, not realistic.[1] I thought the prison courtyard was wonderful, and also the last scene. But people wanted to see it as they had always seen it.

HEYWORTH: Were you yourself happy with the performance?

KLEMPERER: Partly yes, and partly no. I thought that Dülberg's designs were excellent. And the Berlin State Opera Orchestra was very, very good. Rose Pauly sang *Fidelio*; wonderful, really like a boy, but her intonation was not very good. But then Tietjen didn't allow us to take singers from the Linden Opera, where there was Frida Leider, who was naturally much better. Then we gave *The Kiss* by Smetana, conducted by Zemlinsky, and Zweig did Verdi's *Luisa Miller*. Neither of the works was known at that time and neither of them was successful. Then came *Don Giovanni*, which I conducted,[2] and that had more success with the press. At any rate, Einstein, who for me was the most important critic in Berlin, wrote that it was good. But *Don Giovanni* is a very difficult opera. It really needs a revolving stage, and the Kroll didn't have one.

Then, after *Don Giovanni*, came a Stravinsky evening. We gave the first stage performance of *Oedipus Rex*,[3] followed by *Mavra*, which was still virtually unknown,[4] and then *Petrushka*, in that order. For *Oedipus Rex* Dülberg made a wonderful set with a raised amphitheatre for the chorus and the soloists above it. The previous year I had been to the first concert performance of *Oedipus Rex* at the Théâtre Sarah Bernhardt in Paris. Stravinsky himself had conducted, and at that time he really wasn't very good; later on he sometimes conducted splendidly. In rehearsal there was a passage he simply couldn't get right. At the performance I sat next to Jean Cocteau,[5] who was very musical. At one moment it was *comme ci, comme ça*, and Cocteau whispered, "He can't do it. This is impossible." The evening before the performance, there was a reception at the Princess Polignac's and there Stravinsky and Prokofiev played *Oedipus Rex* in a version for four hands. There were a choir, and soloists, but they played the orchestral part on a piano.

HEYWORTH: Did it sound well on the piano?

KLEMPERER: I found it very good. I was more impressed by it then than I was with the whole apparatus in the Théâtre Sarah Bernhardt, and I decided right away to do it myself. Though it wasn't a box office piece and the Volksbühne was very dissatisfied, *Oedipus Rex* was very successful. Of all the modern works we did at the Kroll, it was the one that gave me most pleasure. But the first night was difficult. Almost all the seats had been sold to a trading association that was meeting in Berlin.

[1] Sets were by Ewald Dülberg.   [2] And produced.
[3] Produced by Klemperer.   [4] The first performance in Paris in 1922 had been disastrous.
[5] 1892–1963. Author of text of *Oedipus Rex*.

Naturally, there was only astonishment on the faces of the audience. Still, the press wrote well about it and especially about Dülberg's set.

HEYWORTH: Did Stravinsky come to the Kroll performance?

KLEMPERER: Oh yes, he came to Berlin for the dress rehearsal and the first night.

HEYWORTH: Was he pleased?

KLEMPERER: He also liked Dülberg's set very much, and he has written about it.[1] Naturally, musically, he criticised details—this tempo was a little too slow, and this a little too quick. And then he played me *Apollo Musagetes* on the piano—it was composed but still unperformed. I was delighted by this piece and later on we did it. We did almost everything of Stravinsky's at the Kroll concerts—the Piano Concerto, Capriccio for piano and orchestra, *Les Noces*, *Le Baiser de la fée*. And the *Symphony of Psalms*, naturally.

HEYWORTH: All with the orchestra of the Kroll Opera?

KLEMPERER: Yes. Thank goodness, after the first year Tietjen saw that the two companies, ourselves and the Linden Opera, couldn't function with a single orchestra, as had been intended. So it was divided. I had an excellent leader, Wolfsthal, a Pole. It was a very good orchestra. But easy-going; the players were engaged for life and that's bad—they feel secure and complacent.

HEYWORTH: When did you first meet Stravinsky?

KLEMPERER: In 1914 in Paris. Strauss was conducting the first performance of his *Josefslegende* in a double bill with *Petrushka*, which was conducted by Monteux. *Josefslegende* was very coolly received. But *Petrushka*—that produced storms of applause. It was partly political, of course. It was two months before the war and the French public didn't have as much sympathy for the German Richard Strauss as it did for the Russian ally. But *Josefslegende* is a miserable piece. Very well scored, but . . .

Then later, when I was in Wiesbaden, I wanted to engage Stravinsky as a pianist. His fee was more than the city could afford, but I persuaded some rich people to contribute to it. He played his recently composed Piano Concerto and I conducted. The work made a great impression on me. But at the beginning in rehearsal we had a little misunderstanding. I did the orchestral introduction a little too romantically and Stravinsky said, "No, no. You must think of Savonarola." Then I understood. I conducted *Pulcinella* after the concerto, and I began with two Bach chorales,[2] orchestrated by Schoenberg. I remember that Stravinsky said, "Good, good. These two things of Schoenberg are very good."

HEYWORTH: Is Stravinsky the twentieth-century composer you feel closest to?

KLEMPERER: Yes. I also remained close to the Viennese expressionists. But I'm perhaps more attracted to Stravinsky. For instance, I think his last major work, *Requiem*

[1] *Chroniques de ma vie*, Paris 1935, vol. 2, pp. 109–10.
[2] *Schmücke Dich, O Liebe Seele* and *Komm, Gott, Schöpfer, heiliger Geist*. Both orchestrated in 1922.

Canticles, is wonderful, wonderful. Stravinsky and Schoenberg are the two peaks of music in the first half of the twentieth century. When Stravinsky died I felt we had all lost a great guide. But I found this transfer of his body to Venice absolutely terrible. When one is dead, one is dead. It does not matter where one is buried, does it? For me that is unimportant. When my wife died in Munich, she was naturally buried there, though we lived in Zürich.

During that whole season of 1927–1928 I felt month by month more and more depressed. I couldn't see how to satisfy the Volksbühne, how to fill the house and give worthwhile and rarely performed operas. It was impossible to sleep and I didn't know what to do. Finally, I asked for leave and in the spring of 1928 I went with my wife to a beautiful hotel at Cap d'Antibes. Then came letters from Curjel, to say that Tietjen insisted that I should return to Berlin for a festival to celebrate the reopening of the Linden Opera. I couldn't see why it should be necessary for me to return for that. But I must say that I was already better in every way and I was sleeping again. The Linden Opera reopened with a terrible production of *Die Zauberflöte*, attended by Hindenburg.[1] Curjel told me that the critics had said that the evening was the greatest success the Kroll Opera had had!

HEYWORTH: Did things get easier for the Kroll after the Linden Opera had moved back to its own premises?

KLEMPERER: Yes. Once we were independent, it was much easier. The orchestra was divided. And then the most important thing was that I gave up the position of director, in which I had been responsible for the whole administration as well as the artistic direction. That wasn't for me. I went to Kestenberg and Tietjen and said, "As director, I retire and you must find someone else."

HEYWORTH: But you remained in charge of the whole musical side of the Kroll?

KLEMPERER: Yes, the essential artistic decisions remained mine. As a director they took Ernst Legal, though he also produced, for instance *Das Leben des Orest* by Křenek. I didn't think it was very good. But then the work isn't very good either.

Now that I was delivered of all this administration, I felt better. And then we began the second season, 1928–1929, with *Der fliegende Holländer* and that really was a great success. Moje Forbach was Senta and she was wonderful—today she's an actress. We did the opera more or less in modern dress. Senta wore a sweater and a skirt, nothing else. The sailors were dressed like contemporary sailors, and so was the Dutchman, except that he had a cape. That shocked people enormously. The *Wagnerverein deutscher Frauen*[2] protested about this mockery of Wagner, and before the second performance the police telephoned to say that the Nazis were planning a demonstration; the brown jackets, they were already there. I asked for police protection. Ten detectives sat in the first row of the stalls, and two hundred

[1] Field-Marshal Paul von Beneckendorff und Hindenburg (1847–1934). German President 1925–1934.
[2] The Wagner Association of German Women.

others were posted around the auditorium, and so it came to nothing. Curjel and Legal said that they had never held authority in such high esteem!

By chance Siegfried Wagner[1] was in Berlin at the time and came to the dress rehearsal. Afterwards, he came to see me, and I said to him, "Grüss Gott, Herr Wagner, bitte *entsetzen* Sie sich."[2] He said that the staging looked funny to him. But, musically, I think he found it quite good.

HEYWORTH: Do you think that the Kroll production of *Der fliegende Holländer* had an influence on post-war Bayreuth?

KLEMPERER: I'm convinced of it. We also gave *Die Zauberflöte* with sets by Dülberg and Puccini's three one-acters, *Il Tabarro*, *Suor Angelica* and *Gianni Schicchi*. And then in 1929 we gave the first performance of Hindemith's *Neues vom Tage*. Unfortunately, it wasn't a very good piece, though not as bad as some people said. Hindemith revised it[3] and we then performed it again, but it was hardly any better.

HEYWORTH: Could one say that Hindemith and Stravinsky were more characteristic of the general artistic direction of the Kroll than the Viennese expressionists like Schoenberg and Berg?

KLEMPERER: Yes, I think one could. We did a lot of Hindemith's music in our concerts. We gave the first performance of the Viola Concerto with Hindemith as soloist, and the Cello Concerto,[4] and of course the Konzertmusik for piano, brass and two harps. That we did with Gieseking. He played splendidly. He really was exceptional; his touch was particularly attractive. Unfortunately, afterwards . . . terrible.[5] In November 1931, after the Kroll had shut, I conducted the first performance of Hindemith's oratorio, *Das Unaufhörliche*. The music was good but Gottfried Benn's text was completely incomprehensible.

Ah, you know, the moment in the early twenties when the young Hindemith arrived on the scene with his early quartets and so on, that was splendid. Fresh air and no more pathos. And even his opera *Cardillac*, which he later unfortunately rewrote, much to its disadvantage, that was also full of fresh air. We gave it right away, at the Kroll as well as at Wiesbaden, but of course it wasn't anything for the Volksbühne. I found Hindemith very sympathetic personally. Someone said of him, "Why doesn't Klemperer perform more of your music?" He answered, "Well, he doesn't like it all. That's not a crime."

HEYWORTH: What do you feel about his later music?

[1] Richard Wagner's only son (1869–1930). Ran Bayreuth on highly conservative lines until his death.
[2] A Klemperer pun. "Bitte setzen Sie sich" would mean "Please sit down". "Bitte *ent*setzen Sie sich" means "Please be outraged".
[3] Naturally this does not refer to the subsequent and more thorough-going revision of 1953.
[4] *Kammermusik No. 5*, Opus 36, no. 4 and *Kammermusik No. 3*, Opus 36, no. 2.
[5] A reference to Gieseking's subsequent Nazi sympathies.

KLEMPERER: There are two works written after 1933 I know well and like—the symphony from his opera *Mathis der Maler*, and the ballet, *Nobilissima Visione*. A later work I also like very much is his little opera, *The Long Christmas Dinner*. It's on a text by Thornton Wilder—a wonderful thing. The orchestration is very restrained but well done. I've never heard it; I've only seen the score. Of course there is nothing very surprising in it. It was the young Hindemith who was surprising. It was at this period that Strauss jokingly said to him, "Why do you compose so horribly? You have good ideas." But Hindemith's last years were sad. He fought against the very people who had always supported him. He complained bitterly about the German radio stations, who played everything imaginable, only no Hindemith. He hated the twelve tone system and said that it was unnatural. The tonal relationship of the twelve semi-tones was for him a dogma that couldn't be challenged. It was hard to go along with him in this respect. I heard his last big opera about Kepler, *Die Harmonie der Welt*, in Munich in 1957. Terribly dull! Terribly dull!

Then, after *Neues vom Tage* came the big question of Weill's *Mahagonny*.[1]

HEYWORTH: Why didn't you perform it at the Kroll?

KLEMPERER: Because I didn't like it. Herr Hertzka from Universal Edition came from Vienna and Weill played the opera to Curjel and myself on the piano. Well, I was really a very enthusiastic admirer of *Die Dreigroschenoper*, but *Mahagonny* I found awful. I found it simply a *Schweinerei*. Weill had written an attractive little *Mahagonny*,[2] which had been performed at Baden-Baden.[3] That was delightful. But the opera *Mahagonny* I found obscene. I am not prudish, not at all, but there is a point I can't go beyond. But we did *Der Jasager* at the Kroll—it's for children and was done by children; and also *Der Lindbergh Flug*, a small cantata.

HEYWORTH: Do you then consider Weill's attempt to make a full scale opera out of *Mahagonny* a failure?

KLEMPERER: Completely. I also recently heard a symphony of his on the radio. Absolutely nothing.

HEYWORTH: Why do you think that Weill went to pieces as a composer in America after 1933?

KLEMPERER: He was very interested in money, that's the reason. He got too involved in American show business and all the terrible people in it. Weill's last pieces I find awful. When he arrived in America he gave an interview, in which he described himself as a Tolstoyan. That seemed very strange to us, because only a few months earlier, in Germany, he had seemed to have left-wing sympathies. That didn't

---

[1] *Der Aufstieg und Fall der Stadt Mahagonny* (1930), a full-scale opera that takes as its point of departure the *Mahagonny Songspiel* (1927), otherwise known as *Das kleine Mahagonny*.

[2] The *Songspiel*, first performed in 1927.

[3] To which the Donaueschingen Festival had moved in 1927.

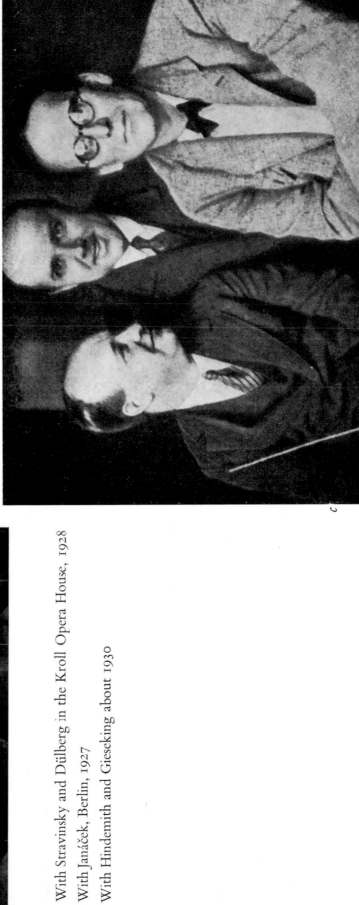

a   With Stravinsky and Dülberg in the Kroll Opera House, 1928

b   With Janáček, Berlin, 1927

c   With Hindemith and Gieseking about 1930

a

b

c

d

a *left to right:* Bruno Walter, Toscanini, Erich Kleiber, Otto Klemperer and Wilhelm Furtwängler at a reception for Toscanini in Berlin in 1929

b With Schoenberg, Webern and Scherchen in Donaueschingen in 1924

c Leningrad, 1925

d With Artur Schnabel about 1933

impress us very much. Anyway, instead of Weill's *Mahagonny*, we did Křenek's *Das Leben des Orest*.

HEYWORTH: Was that an improvement?

KLEMPERER: No, it was a dilution.[1] But it wasn't so aggressive. Anyway, we did it and it was quite successful. I'd be interested to know what you think about Křenek. He's not without talent. He began with a piece that made him world-famous, *Jonny spielt auf*. Then at the Kroll we gave three one-acters, *Das heimliche Königsreich*[2]—that was a little too secretive for me, *Schwergewicht*, which is absolutely operetta-like, and *Der Diktator*, which I found a very good opera. *Das Leben des Orest*, which we also did, is a curious mixture of old and new—not so good, but also not so bad. But there's a delightfully parodistic piece of his I've conducted, the *Kleine Sinfonie*.

HEYWORTH: You also did a Schoenberg double-bill.

KLEMPERER: Yes. That was in 1929–1930. Zemlinsky conducted *Erwartung* and I conducted *Die glückliche Hand*. Personally, I find *Erwartung* much the better of the two; *Die glückliche Hand* seems to me a failure. The text is awful and then there are complicated lighting instructions in the score: every scene has to have a different colour. We didn't follow the instructions in the score so exactly, and I think we were right to do so.

HEYWORTH: Was Schoenberg satisfied with the production?

KLEMPERER: He spoke very nicely about the musical performance, but scenically it didn't please him at all.[3] But then he had no idea of theatre, really none at all. A wonderful man, but . . . It was right in a cultural sense to give these works at the Kroll. In another way it was nonsense. I never saw the theatre so empty. What should a simple member of the Volksbühne have thought of *Erwartung* and *Die glückliche Hand*?

HEYWORTH: I imagine that was one of the basic problems at the Kroll?

KLEMPERER: Yes, because the Kroll Opera depended on a contract with the Volksbühne, and its subscribers didn't want things like *Erwartung* and *Die glückliche Hand*. In general we had a very good public reaction, especially from young people. And also from the intellectual world; men like Einstein, Bloch and Walter Benjamin came regularly and that was good for us. But the Volksbühne wanted big singers, big arias, big applause and so on. The two other opera houses had better voices than we did. Our singers were limited, though some of them were very good. We did in fact give popular operas like *Carmen*, *The Tales of Hoffman* and *Butterfly*. But naturally we didn't give them in conventional productions. We gave

[1] Another Klemperer pun. Improvement=Verbesserung. Watering down=Verwässerung.
[2] *The Secret Kingdom.*
[3] In a letter of 14 September 1930, to Legal, Schoenberg gave detailed instructions for the production of both works. See *The Works of Arnold Schoenberg* by Josef Rufer, pp. 35–6.

Der fliegende Holländer, but it wasn't the Volksbühne's *Fliegende Holländer*.
Dülberg became ill with tuberculosis and we brought in other designers.
Schlemmer,[1] Strnad[2] and Moholy-Nagy[3] —all very progressive men, too progressive to please the authorities. "Die ganze Richtung passt mir nicht",[4] as the Kaiser used to say. In the same way that was already the reaction of Nazi circles to the Kroll.

Sometimes I think we went too far. For instance, in *The Tales of Hoffmann* in the barcarolle one feels the movement of the music. But Moholy-Nagy, who did the sets, wanted two nearly naked girls on a swing, swinging in time with the music. Supposedly a new way for opera!

Once I returned from a vacation and in a rehearsal of Auber's *La muette de Portici* found the whole scene covered in a red flag. I disagreed. I thought it was not right, because the tragedy is more the tragedy of the dumb woman than the tragedy of the Italian people. They also gave a *Barber of Seville*—of today! Now that is not possible. The production was well thought out, but it's very difficult to play a piece of this sort in modern dress. In fact Tietjen stopped the production until it was changed. Curjel fought for it. I was silent.

Then came the morning in 1930 when Herr Tietjen appeared in our office and said quite casually that the Kroll Opera would be shut the following year.[5] We thought that he had gone mad. I did everything I could to save it. I wrote an article, "In eigener Sache",[6] in the *Berliner Tageblatt*. As I didn't know what else to do in Berlin, I went to see Pacelli,[7] the Secretary of State at the Vatican: I happened to have a concert in Rome just at that time. He was very musical, understood me at once and was very ready to help. He advised me to go to Dr Brüning,[8] the German Chancellor, and Prälat Kaas, the leader of the Zentrum Party.[9]

A conversation with Kaas was pretty fruitless. But my meeting with Brüning

---

[1] Oskar Schlemmer (1888–1943). Head of department of theatrical design at the Bauhaus.

[2] Oskar Strnad (1879–1935). Austrian architect and stage designer.

[3] Laszlo Moholy-Nagy (1895–1946). Hungarian painter and "constructionist". Taught at the Bauhaus 1922–1928 and founded the New Bauhaus in Chicago.

[4] Literally, "The whole direction does not suit me." A favourite expression of Wilhelm II, when anything displeased him.

[5] Tietjen's prognosis was correct. The Kroll Opera shut in July 1931.

[6] Literally, "In one's own cause".

[7] Eugenio Pacelli (1876–1958). Papal Nuncio in Berlin 1927–1929, during which period Klemperer had got to know him. Secretary of State at the Vatican 1930–1939. Pope Pius XII 1939–1958.

[8] Heinrich Brüning (1885–1970). German Chancellor 1930–1932. Member of the Zentrum Party.

[9] The Catholic party of the centre. At the crucial period it held the balance in the Prussian Landtag. When it transferred its support from the Social Democrats, who were in favour of the Kroll Opera, to the parties of the right, which were opposed to it on ideological as well as economic grounds, the theatre's position was fatally undermined.

was very revealing. He told me that he would like to help but couldn't. He said, "I cannot help you because Germany has not paid her war debts. Instead of that she has rebuilt the Linden Opera. That should not have happened. That is why I am pleased that at least the Kroll Opera is to be shut." I later met Brüning on another occasion and realised that he was a sensitive and understanding man. But it was a scandal that this theatre, which cost the state the least money, should have been closed. Naturally, it was political. People saw in us a danger and that's why we were closed so quickly.

HEYWORTH: Yes, but couldn't one say that, in the middle of the economic crisis at that time, it was difficult for Berlin to maintain three opera houses? And which was to be shut? It seems to me to have been a very difficult situation.

KLEMPERER: None of them should have been shut. We had already existed for four years. I mean, there were possibilities. Together with Dr Curjel, who occasionally deputised for Legal as director, I planned a fourth season to prove that the Kroll was artistically necessary and able to survive, that to shut it would be a monstrous step. In that last season of 1930–1931, we gave eight productions—Charpentier's *Louise*, Gluck's *Iphigenia in Tauris*, *Figaro*, Schoenberg's *Erwartung* and *Die glückliche Hand*, *Falstaff Butterfly*, Offenbach's *La Périchole*, and Janáček's *From the House of the Dead*—a powerful repertory. It was a very worthy finish. Yet this theatre, which cost less money than either of Berlin's other two opera houses, was brutally and arbitrarily shut against the will of the public.

It was just a matter of good will, and there was distinctly bad will. The Kroll was not shut for financial but for political reasons. The authorities did not like our whole direction. They did not like us. When I went to say farewell to Tietjen in 1933, I said to him, "Naturally the Nazis are very much against me because I am a Jew." He said, "No, that is not so important. It's your whole political and artistic direction they don't like. That is the reason why the Kroll Opera was closed."

HEYWORTH: Can one speak of a Kroll style?

KLEMPERER: Yes.

HEYWORTH: How would you describe it?

KLEMPERER: To give good opera performances. We gave classical works with an open mind. We gave works of living composers. We weren't interested in so much pomp and spectacle.

HEYWORTH: Do you think that the fact that you didn't have much money to play with worked out positively from an artistic point of view?

KLEMPERER: It was a positive thing that wasn't intended by the authorities! But it *was* positive, because not having much money to spend forced us away from an old-fashioned naturalism. In this respect our style was a forerunner of the world of Wieland Wagner.

HEYWORTH: Do you feel you succeeded at the Kroll?

KLEMPERER: No. It was only a beginning. The Kroll only lasted for four years and you can't build a palace in four years. It was a beginning.

HEYWORTH: What productions at the Kroll do you look back on with most pride?

KLEMPERER: In my opinion the most artistically successful were *Fidelio*, *Oedipus Rex*, *Der fliegende Holländer* and *Figaro*.

HEYWORTH: Dr Klemperer, when you look back, would you say that the years at the Kroll were artistically the most important in your life?

KLEMPERER: Yes. Yes, I would.

HEYWORTH: And then you went to the Linden Opera?

KLEMPERER: In my contract it stated that, should the Kroll Opera be shut, Herr Klemperer is contracted to work in the same capacity in the Linden Opera. In the same capacity! Very well then. The Kroll Opera was shut and there my position as I understood it, had been that of *Generalmusikdirektor* with full powers, who selected the operas he wanted to conduct, and did not only do what he was told to do. The Intendant, Tietjen, was of another opinion. He insisted that it was for him to decide what I should do.

And so it came to an action before the *Arbeitsgericht*,[1] where you cannot have a lawyer, but have to argue your own case. I spoke at length about the difference between the function as opposed to the mere title of *Generalmusikdirektor*. For instance, Friedrich Wilhelm IV gave Mendelssohn the title, though he was only rarely in Berlin. In my case it was a matter of the function. I said that the tribunal reminded me of the tribunal which sent Dreyfus to Devil's Island and that for me the Linden Opera was Devil's Island. I lost spectacularly, because there is little you can do against the Prussian state, and I had to pay 5,000 marks as a result.

When I saw Tietjen at the beginning of the next season, he proposed that we should simply forget my old contract and make a new one, whereby I would only be available during special periods. But there was a deeper reason for that: he wanted to get rid of me. So I refused. Then he tried absolutely to force me into the repertory. He said, "Next week you will conduct *Die Walküre*." I said, "How many rehearsals?" "No rehearsals." "Thank you, without me." But my contract gave me no basis for refusing to conduct and for several weeks the horrible apparition of this *Walküre* confronted me. But it came to nothing. Chance? There is no chance, says Schiller.[2]

I felt miserable at the Linden Opera and longed to be back at the Kroll. But in fact they couldn't give me the same position as I'd had at the Kroll because Kleiber, Furtwängler[3] and Leo Blech were all there. There were too many

---

[1] Labour tribunal.

[2] In *Wallenstein's Tod*.

[3] Wilhelm Furtwängler (1886–1954). Had at that time no position at the Linden Opera, but conducted there occasionally.

conductors. But at least I was able to insist that in the two years[1] I was at the Linden Opera I only conducted productions that had been taken over from the Kroll or were new.

HEYWORTH: What did you conduct there?

KLEMPERER: *Der Rosenkavalier*, absolutely new; *Così fan tutte*, also new; and from the Kroll we took over *Falstaff* with the same singers, and *Figaro*. *Der Rosenkavalier* was produced by Gründgens and I didn't like it at all. We also did *Così fan tutte* with Gründgens. He had produced *Figaro* very well at the Kroll, and so I asked him to do *Così fan tutte*, but that was very bad. He didn't understand it properly.

Then at the end I conducted *Tannhäuser*. That was especially remarkable, because the first night was on February 12 1933,[2] the eve of the fiftieth anniversary of Wagner's death. At the beginning everything went very calmly, but when I appeared at the beginning of the third act there began a ridiculous noise, as my supporters applauded and others whistled and shouted. It lasted at least ten to fifteen minutes. I sat quietly and then I started to conduct.

The press reaction was awful—I don't know why. Fehling did a severely stylised production, very much with my support. Oskar Strnad's sets were very good.[3] In the second act we divided the scenery on a moving stage so that the first scene could be more intimate than the latter part of the act. Tietjen was in a strange position, because at Bayreuth[4] he could not dare anything like this. He said to me, "I can't allow here what I forbid in Bayreuth." I said, "Of course you can't." Well, then I went on leave to Italy and Hungary, and when I came back *Tannhäuser* was still in the repertory, but in the old production, with sets by some hack theatrical designer.

I went to Tietjen. He said, "It's no longer any business of yours. Unfortunately, I cannot employ you further."

"Really. And what is to happen to the Ninth Symphony?" (I still had a concert scheduled).

"Someone else will have to do that."

"There will be a scandal."

Tietjen replied, "Permit me, there will be no scandal. And if there is one, that doesn't disturb me. This government knows when there is going to be a scandal." Naturally, after those courageous words the concert didn't take place.

HEYWORTH: When was that?

KLEMPERER: In March 1933. I was in a dreamlike condition. At the time of the Reichstag fire in February I hadn't been able to believe what I later realised had

[1] 1931–1933.
[2] The Nazis had come to power less than a fortnight earlier, on 30 January 1933.
[3] Said to have been subsequently destroyed on Hitler's express instructions.
[4] Tietjen had become artistic director of Bayreuth in 1931.

happened, that a German government could burn down its own parliament. Then came the *Berufsbeamtengesetz*,[1] which finally brought my activity in Germany to an end. That decreed that no one of alien race might occupy a position as a civil servant. Civil servants had to be of German blood, and as a conductor at the Berlin State Opera I was a civil servant.

HEYWORTH: Did Tietjen make no attempt to keep you? Because Blech,[2] for instance, remained in Germany and even conducted for a number of years.

KLEMPERER: On the contrary. It is so funny that I must tell you. On April 3 I went to see Georg Klemperer, who lived nearby, and he told me, "Just imagine, this morning they arrested the neurologist, Goldstein." He was a famous doctor, but he was a Jew—that was the reason. "Where is he?" I asked. "Nobody knows." "Doesn't his wife know either?" "No." I thought, my goodness, it is time to leave, otherwise the same thing will happen to me. The next morning I went with my son to his school in Grunewald[3] and told the headmaster that he wouldn't be coming any more. Then I went to the police to get my passport stamped with a permit to travel. And then I went to say good-bye to Tietjen.

I had to do that. After all, he was my boss. I told him that I was leaving. He replied that I couldn't take a vacation.

"I don't mean a vacation, I'm leaving." In other words I was telling him that I was not coming back.

Then he asked, "Well, where are you going?"

"I'm going to Zürich. I can be in Berlin in twelve hours if you need me."

"And where are you staying in Zürich?"

"I'm going to the Bircher-Benner." That's a little sanatorium with special diets, vegetarian diet or mixed diet, and so on.

Then Tietjen asked me, "Which diet are you taking?"

"I prefer mixed diet."

"Yes, perhaps that's better."

We spoke like this for some minutes and then I said, "My train goes at half past two. I must go."

"All right. Good-bye."

Imagine, this man knew I didn't have a penny in my pocket and that I would never come back. And he was only interested in diets. Terrible, terrible.

[1] A decree concerning the employment of officials, promulgated by the Nazi government.
[2] It is supposed that Blech's presence at the Berlin State Opera was tolerated by the Nazis until 1937 for the obscure reason that he had been appointed *Generalmusikdirektor* by the Kaiser.
[3] A suburb of Berlin.

CHAPTER V

Schoenberg and the Years of Emigration

KLEMPERER: My wife brought me to the Anhalter Station. In the train from Berlin to Basle there were almost only Jews. I had the feeling that I would be arrested at the frontier, and the Jews as they crossed the Red Sea cannot have been happier than I was when I found myself on Swiss soil and free. Fourteen days later my wife came with the children and brought—oh, miracle—money, which she had cunningly baked into a cake. Two weeks later came our housekeeper, who had packed up our flat in Berlin. So we were all together again.

HEYWORTH: Did you then go to America?

KLEMPERER: Not directly. In the course of the summer I travelled to Rome to see Pacelli and ask for help for the Jews. He told me that the Church had already been asked for help from many sides, but that I should never forget that the Jewish and the Catholic ways were different. I understood. He arranged an audience for me with the Pope.[1] But beforehand he asked me not to touch on politics. His Holiness didn't like that!

That summer I conducted Bartók's Second Piano Concerto in Vienna with him as soloist. That was a great experience for me. He was a wonderful pianist and musician. The beauty of his tone, the energy and lightness of his playing were un-forgettable. It was almost painfully beautiful. He played with great freedom, that was what was so wonderful. He was a strange man—very reserved, very shy, but very sympathetic. He had a new wife at that time. But the old also came to the rehearsal, so he appeared with two wives.

Later that summer I met by chance an American woman in Florence. She said, "I hear you have some trouble in Germany. Would you like to come to Los Angeles? We need a new conductor. If you would like to come, I will send a telegram to my friend on the committee." Well that was wonderful, so I said, "Of course."

[1] Pius XI.

Arthur Judson[1] was my agent and there was a long discussion about salary. I thought it was too small. Judson said that Los Angeles could not pay more. Then I agreed and, after some concerts in Vienna and Salzburg, in October 1933 I went to America, not by aeroplane—that hardly existed at the time—but by boat. I was very glad to have this position, because the winter was taken care of.

HEYWORTH: What was the orchestra like?

KLEMPERER: Very good. Not as good as the Boston or the Philadelphia Orchestra, but very good. It had a lot of routine, and sight-reading was no difficulty. I conducted every two weeks and the concerts were all very well attended.

HEYWORTH: Was it possible to do new works?

KLEMPERER: I was able to do Bruckner's Fourth and Seventh Symphonies, *Das Lied von der Erde* and also Stravinsky. All that was new to Los Angeles. Forty years ago, there was no Stockhausen and no Boulez.

HEYWORTH: And Schoenberg? Wasn't he also in Los Angeles at this time?

KLEMPERER: Yes, though he only came to California in 1935. Schoenberg first went to Paris, where he formally returned to the Jewish religion.[2] When he first came to America, he was at a little east-coast conservatory. Then, because the climate there was bad for him, he came to Los Angeles.

At first he was furious because I didn't perform him more. I constantly tried to explain that the Los Angeles public was not yet ready for him. I did his Bach E flat Prelude and Fugue. Then he wrote a little suite[3] for students in the antique style, with a gavotte and a minuet and so on, and I did that. Later, I urged him to write something like a transcription, and he arranged Brahms's G minor piano quartet for full orchestra—a wonderful thing. That's rarely performed here in Europe—as good as not at all. I would like to do it again; it sounds marvellous. One doesn't want to hear the original quartet, the transcription is so much more beautiful.

HEYWORTH: But you had difficulties with him over it, didn't you?

KLEMPERER: Everyone had difficulties with Schoenberg, that wasn't anything unusual! Well, he instrumented the Brahms and then he said he must have his fee straightaway, before the performance, because he had to send the manuscript to Vienna, where a relative of his would copy it. I told him that it wasn't really customary to pay a composer before a performance. But Schoenberg demanded three hundred dollars—not as an advance, but for sending the score to Vienna. I didn't want trouble, so I gave him a cheque on my own account. I told him that I couldn't ask

[1] 1881—. President of Columbia Concerts Corporation. Also manager of the New York Philharmonic Orchestra 1922–1956, and of the Philadelphia Orchestra 1915–1936.

[2] Schoenberg, who had had a Catholic upbringing, had become a Protestant at the age of eighteen.

[3] *Suite in the old style for string orchestra* (1934). At the bottom of the title page of the manuscript is a note in red pencil: "The spots on this score are Klemperer's drops of sweat." Klemperer gave the first performance on 18 May 1935.

the manager for it, he would think me mad, and that this was the only way of settling the difficulty. "Yes," he said, "You've done the only possible thing." Then he said to me, "You won't be angry if I give the first performance to New York?" I was angry, though finally the New York concert fell through, so I gave the first performance after all.[1]

That was the "quarrel" I had with him. Otherwise, we were good neighbours. I remember that when I did *Das Lied von der Erde* he came to all the rehearsals and gave me advice. But I must tell you a nice story. When we played his Brahms transcription, the manager of the Los Angeles orchestra said, "I don't know why people say that Schoenberg has no melodies. That was very melodic."

I really am proud that I was able to help him to get a position at the University of California, Los Angeles.[2] When I was a guest conductor with the New York Philharmonic I heard that a member of the music department had died and I cabled, urging them to take Schoenberg. Of course in a way it was nonsense. In America everyone studies music, but not in Schoenberg's conception of study. Law students, medical students, they all learn a violin or some other instrument. And there are student orchestras—sometimes even quite good. But of course when Schoenberg analysed Beethoven's Ninth Symphony they didn't understand. He also gave private lessons, but only a few of these. He was miserably paid, and finally he got a shabby pension. *Schweinerei*. I was often with him. He never felt himself sufficiently recognised; he always felt neglected. If he had lived he would hardly have believed that *Moses und Aron* would be performed. I heard it twice here in Zürich.[3] It's a splendid work and there are many fine things in it. But as a whole it doesn't move me so much. I think one must hear it twenty times, before one really understands its basic conception.

Schoenberg was a strange man. He could be very nice and he could be very, very impolite. When I was in Australia in 1949, I conducted his *Theme and Variations* —I think it was first written for military band and only later for orchestra.[4] I told him that I had performed it three times. He said, "All right." Nothing else. The difference between those two giants, Stravinsky and Schoenberg, was unbelievable. Stravinsky was very polite and very nice, Schoenberg could be abominable (laughter). But when I absolutely wanted to pay for lessons I had with him, he refused. He said, "No, I don't take payment from a colleague." It was very good of him.

HEYWORTH: Why did you take lessons with Schoenberg?

[1] 7 May 1938, in Los Angeles.
[2] Schoenberg was appointed professor of music at UCLA in 1936. Compelled to resign at the age of seventy in 1944, he received a pension of $38 a month.
[3] First performed there 6 June 1957.
[4] Opus 43a and b.

KLEMPERER: My God, because he was a very good teacher! I was happy that he was in Los Angeles and I wanted to take advantage of that. His lessons were very interesting. He never said a word about the twelve-tone system. Not a word. He looked through what I had written, he corrected it in a very wise manner, and we analysed Bach motets, but no so-called modern music.

In my opinion the great thing that Schoenberg taught us is that there is no real difference between consonance and dissonance. The idea of composing with twelve tones is very fascinating. I have used it. It's not just an abstract idea. Opponents always say, "It's not music, it's mathematics." That's not true; it *can* be music. Naturally, if it is used only in a mathematical way, it isn't music. Used in the right way, the system can express a composer's intentions. I find one of Schoenberg's last works among the strongest pieces I know and it's written purely in the twelve-tone system.[1] I think Schoenberg sometimes went a little far, as in his ban on repeating notes. That's a hard rule, which one can't always stick to—at least I can't. But the basic idea is wonderful. It has freed us from tonality. Wonderful!

But today Schoenberg is a classic. I mean, Pierre Boulez has written, "Schoenberg est mort."[2] Modern music isn't any longer concerned with the twelve-tone system. Today they make noises with the strings of the piano and stamp with their feet and that is supposed to be music. It isn't! But I don't put Stockhausen in that category. I heard his *Gruppen* for three orchestras in London in 1968. That made a great impression on me. There are really fantastic things in it—I didn't know such sounds existed.

HEYWORTH: What about other composers of his generation? Boulez for instance?

KLEMPERER: I can't say that I think that everything of Boulez's is good. But I admire the *Sonatina for flute and piano*. That's a delightful piece. *Le Marteau sans maître* I think is *passé*. I mean, that's pure expressionism. It's not a new style or a new form —it follows Schoenberg. As for the bigger things like *Pli selon pli*, which I have heard on records, I must hear them more often. But I think highly of him. The most recent thing of his I heard, *Domaine*, I didn't like much. But that doesn't mean anything. I'm not competent to discuss these avant-gardists. I was born and brought up with classical music. My own music sounds different from Haydn, of course, because this is the twentieth century. But it's based on tonality, whereas avant-gardists like Boulez and Stockhausen write atonal, anti-tonal music.

When I am asked what I think about modern music, I can only say, "What is modern?" I only know good and bad music, strong and weak music. I would like to emphasise that to my ears "modern" is a dreadful word. It reminds me of "mode". For me, what counts is quality.

[1] The String Trio of 1946.
[2] Essay first published in *The Score*, May 1952.

HEYWORTH: When did you first meet Schoenberg?

KLEMPERER: I think in 1911 in Munich. I met him with Zemlinsky, when Zemlinsky was conducting some Offenbach produced by Reinhardt. I had written a little stage music for Reinhardt's production of the *Oresteia*. It wasn't very good and Schoenberg was . . . well, not very pleased with it. At this period he seemed to me very proud and distant.

Then I heard *Pierrot Lunaire* in Hamburg. That was very soon after its first performance in Berlin.[1] It made a profound impression on me. I hadn't heard anything like it. I still love it, only the poems are impossible today. I find them terribly exaggerated—"die blaue Wäscherin" and so on. I would like to conduct it, but without the texts.

I talked to Schoenberg in Hamburg, and I told him, "When I read your *Five Orchestral Pieces*,[2] I don't hear them. I mean, with other music I hear what I read, but in this case I don't. I can count the bars, but that's not enough." He replied, "Yes, it is enough—for the moment." And in a certain sense he was right. For instance, in the first years no one could sing the chorus of the five Jews in *Salome* correctly. But when Strauss heard it, he said, "It's all right. In time it will come." And today they sing it without difficulty.

HEYWORTH: Did you like Schoenberg's other early works?

KLEMPERER: I remember that, when I came to give my first concert with the Berlin Philharmonic about 1920, I gave *Verklärte Nacht* and *Pelléas et Mélisande* and nothing else. *Pelléas* isn't Schoenberg's greatest work, not at all. Then, as I told you, we did *Erwartung* and *Die glückliche Hand* at the Kroll and in a concert I did his film music[3]—a very, very good piece. I also gave his transcription of Bach's E flat prelude and fugue.[4] Do you know that? Very interesting—for an enormous orchestra. Then he composed his opera *Von Heute auf Morgen*,[5] and naturally he wanted the Kroll to give it right away. I couldn't; it's complicated beyond all measure.

HEYWORTH: Did you feel close to his music? Did it seem to you of quite special importance?

KLEMPERER: I waited. I waited and hoped that a piece would come to which I could say, "Yes".

HEYWORTH: What pieces would you say "Yes" to now?

KLEMPERER: Perhaps the little piece of film music. *Pierrot Lunaire* is, after all these years, very strange. The music is extraordinary, but the text . . . *Die glückliche Hand* I find an awful piece. To *Erwartung* I can say without any reserve; it's a

---

[1] 16 October 1912.   [2] Completed 1909, first performed by Henry Wood in London in 1912.
[3] *Begleitungsmusik zu einer Lichtspielszene* (*Accompaniment to a film scene*) (1930). Klemperer gave the first performance.
[4] 1928.   [5] Completed 1 January 1929.

tragic work of genius. Of his chamber music for my taste the best thing is the String Trio—a wonderful work, perhaps the most important work of his I know. But I don't have very strong feeling for the Piano Concerto or the Violin Concerto.

HEYWORTH: What about Webern's music?

KLEMPERER: I don't understand it. I know it, of course. I conducted his symphony in Berlin, as well as in Vienna. But I couldn't find my way into it. I found it terribly boring. So I asked Webern—I was staying in Vienna—to come and play it to me on the piano. Then perhaps I would understand it better. He came and played every note with enormous intensity and fanaticism.

HEYWORTH: Not coolly?

KLEMPERER: No, passionately! When he had finished, I said, "You know, I cannot conduct it in that way. I'm simply not able to bring that enormous intensity to your music. I must do as well as I can." I did so, and it went quite well. I think that Webern was happy when anyone played his music at that time—that was about 1931. And I am sure that he was a very good musician. Stravinsky had the greatest admiration for him. He said something to the effect that for us Webern is an extract of genius. But I don't believe that. I think that Webern's music is perhaps a sign of the time of crisis in which it appeared. I also believe in his absolute integrity. But that I was very eager to conduct his music, that I can't say.

HEYWORTH: Did you go to America with your family?

KLEMPERER: In 1933 I went alone. I sent my wife and children to Vienna, because I wrongly imagined that Hitler wouldn't invade Austria. That turned out to be a mistake on my part. The Los Angeles season ended in spring and in summer the orchestra gives concerts in the Hollywood Bowl, an open-air auditorium. I didn't want to do these. It's not very dignified and there is only one rehearsal for each concert. In any case, the orchestra's economic situation was very uncertain. I said I would return in winter if it wanted me, but that I would spend the summer in Europe as I wanted to be with my family. In Vienna I found that conditions had become much worse. Dollfuss was murdered while I was there.[1] It looked constantly blacker. So in 1935 my family and I all finally went to America, and we settled in Los Angeles, where I had been engaged for three years. Five years later I became an American citizen.

In the season of 1934–1935 I had been invited by Judson to conduct for four weeks in New York and I think for eight weeks in Philadelphia, so that, together with Los Angeles, I was well occupied. In New York I conducted Hindemith's symphony from *Mathis der Maler*, which was absolutely new at the time.[2]

[1] Engelbert Dollfuss, Austrian Chancellor 1892–1934. Murdered by the Nazis in an attempted *Putsch* in July 1934.

[2] First performed in Berlin by Furtwängler on 12 March 1934, an occasion that brought about a crisis in the relationship of Furtwängler to the Nazi regime.

HEYWORTH: Was that the first time you had conducted in New York?

KLEMPERER: No. I had been in New York much earlier, in 1926, when I had conducted Damrosch's[1] orchestra, the New York Symphony Orchestra, not the New York Philharmonic, which was the leading orchestra.

In 1936 I had the great honour to be asked to stand in for Toscanini with the New York Philharmonic during the first three months of the season. Toscanini had written to say that he wouldn't be coming until January. But you know, it was terrible. On Thursday one had the first concert. Then it was repeated on Friday afternoon. That's possible. But then to have another concert on Saturday with a partially changed programme, and then on Sunday a radio concert for the whole of America—that's really too much.

HEYWORTH: How did Toscanini put up with it?

KLEMPERER: I don't know. I don't know.

HEYWORTH: Working in New York wasn't much pleasure?

KLEMPERER: Oh, no. Firstly, the orchestra was really not so good; Boston was much better. And I was only too eager to do something big, like a Mahler symphony. Judson said, "That's not possible. There won't even be a hundred people in the auditorium." And in a certain sense he was right; at that time Mahler was quite down. Finally, he agreed to *Das Lied von der Erde*, if we could find a couple of singers who would bring in the public. It turned out that they couldn't be found, so I said I wanted to do Mahler's Second Symphony. He said, "Mr Klemperer, I advise you not to do it. It will result in a big deficit." I insisted and it was an enormous success, also with the critics. But the next day I got a letter from Judson, saying that, as he had warned me, there was a deficit of five thousand dollars on the concert.

Then Toscanini announced that, though he would return that January, it would be the last time that he would come to New York.[2] Of course, I had hopes that I would be the first to be considered as his successor. But I knew that after this affair of the Mahler symphony I wouldn't be engaged again.

There was a move to get Furtwängler. In fact it was almost arranged. But then Ira Hirschmann,[3] a business man, who was also the founder of a series of chamber concerts, gave an interview in *The New York Times* in which he said that if Staatsrat Furtwängler[4] was engaged, that would be a slap in the face of all New

[1] Walter Damrosch (1862–1950). Director of the New York Symphony Orchestra in the 1920s. The society that ran it had been founded by his father, Leopold Damrosch.

[2] Toscanini was conductor for the Philharmonic Symphony Orchestra from 1927 to 1936. From 1937 to 1954 he was conductor of the National Broadcasting Corporation Symphony Orchestra.

[3] 1901—. Founder (1946) and president of "New Friends of Music". Also co-author with Artur Schnabel of *Reflections on Music*.

[4] Furtwängler had received this title, which had been invented by Goering, in 1933. By 1936 he had partially composed his differences with the Nazi regime.

York Jews, and he and his friends would withdraw their subscriptions. That worried Arthur Judson. And then Furtwängler sent a telegram, saying that he would not come until the American people had learnt the difference between art and politics. So they took Barbirolli. How that came about, I don't know. Anyway they treated him worse than he deserved. He wasn't so bad, even if he wasn't so good either. But they attacked him terribly in America.

HEYWORTH: It wasn't a very enviable position, to be Toscanini's successor.

KLEMPERER: Judson always said, "This Toscanini is going to ruin our business, because he's the only conductor who draws the public."

I conducted a lot in the American provinces at that period. Out of the blue, I got a letter from Pittsburgh to say that they wanted to found an orchestra and to ask whether I would like to take part in establishing it and conduct the opening concerts. Certainly, I answered, and I did in fact do so. Then they offered me the position of permanent conductor. But I couldn't bring myself to accept. I preferred to remain in California, and so they took Reiner—a good conductor.

HEYWORTH: Did you conduct any opera in America?

KLEMPERER: No, nothing.

HEYWORTH: Did you miss that very much?

KLEMPERER: Very much. But the Metropolitan didn't seem to want me. At any rate, the director, Johnson, never approached me. Then when I was asked, I was ill and couldn't accept.

HEYWORTH: How did you take to life in America?

KLEMPERER: I felt in the wrong place. The orchestras in the East are good, technically. But one cannot compare them with, for instance, the Vienna Philharmonic. You know, with all those Central European refugees in California—Heinrich and Thomas Mann, Kortner, Brecht, Dessau, Reinhardt, Eisler—intellectual life was very lively. But none of them remained. When peace came they all returned to Europe. Only Stravinsky and Schoenberg stayed.

HEYWORTH: Did you find the programmes in America very dependent on box office receipts?

KLEMPERER: Yes. On one occasion in Los Angeles I was asked to end Tchaikovsky's *Symphonie pathétique* with the third movement, the electrifying march. The manager wanted me to leave out the marvellous last movement. Naturally, I didn't do so.

In Los Angeles I also experienced the limits of freedom in America, which is always talking about freedom. In 1935 or 1936 I had to dismiss a number of musicians, simply because they were too old, and I engaged others, whom I had auditioned behind a curtain. The next day the orchestra's president sent for me. He said, "I hear you have dismissed some musicians."

"Yes."

"And have engaged some new musicians."

"Yes."

"No more Jews, I hope."

"I left Berlin for that reason. Am I back in Berlin?"

"I'm not an anti-Semite. I play bridge with a Jew every week."

HEYWORTH: What about American composers? Did any interest you? What about Aaron Copland?

KLEMPERER: His music didn't impress me. *El Salón México* I even find awful. Pooh, I don't like that. The composer who was important was Gershwin.

HEYWORTH: What sort of an impression did he make?

KLEMPERER: A cheeky fellow.[1] The Los Angeles orchestra was in financial difficulties, and Oscar Levant—he was a pupil of Schoenberg—said, "Give a concert with Gershwin. That will be full to bursting point." I said, "I've never conducted anything of his, but I'd be glad to do so. Bring us together." So a lunch was arranged. There Gershwin said, "I don't know whether you command the style of my music." Quite *de haute en bas*. I said, "I don't know either, but I've managed with Beethoven, so it will probably be all right." It came to nothing. He was very, very arrogant; but very gifted. *Porgy and Bess* is more than attractive.

HEYWORTH: When did you become ill in America?

KLEMPERER: In 1938. I began to suffer from frightful disturbances of balance and a brain tumour was finally diagnosed. It may be that it originated in a fall I had at Leipzig in 1933. I was to conduct *Ein Heldenleben* and at the rehearsal I carelessly leant against the railings of the podium and the next thing I knew was that I was lying on the floor. It was quite a drop. I was unconscious for some minutes and I suffered concussion. The doctors thought that that might have been the beginning of the tumour.

I was in danger of my life and I was advised to go to Boston for an operation. I had it in the autumn of 1939 and it went relatively well. But for some time afterwards things weren't so easy. I was four months in hospital and then had to remain for a longer time in an hotel under medical supervision. I spent some time in New York with friends and then returned to Los Angeles. Even today I don't really know why Los Angeles dissolved my contract. Perhaps they didn't trust my health. In the following years things went very badly for us financially. I couldn't take a regular position. I conducted a very, very little. No one invited me.

Finally in 1946 I returned to Europe for a concert tour accompanied by my wife. My first concert was in Stockholm, and then there was a festival in Interlaken, where I conducted the Amsterdam Concertgebouw Orchestra. Everyone seemed pleased to see me. A member of the orchestra's committee said that now I was back again, they all felt that the war was over. That was very nice to hear.

[1] In the original, "Ein frecher Hund".

In Stockholm I met Aladar Toth, the husband of Annie Fischer. He wasn't a practising musician, but a musicologist, and for many years he had been music critic of *Pester Lloyd*, the German paper in Budapest. In 1947 I made a second European tour with my daughter and in Salzburg I got a letter from Toth. In the meantime he had become director of the Budapest Opera and he offered me a big position. I accepted and in the winter of that year I went there. My wife and daughter followed later.

HEYWORTH: What was the attraction of Budapest?

KLEMPERER: I was glad to be able to conduct opera, which I hadn't done since 1933, apart from *Figaro* at the Salzburg Festival of 1947 and *Don Giovanni* the same year in Vienna. And then I had three good orchestras at my disposal. In 1933, when I had been in Budapest, I had found the sound of the strings of the concert orchestra quite exceptional. They were almost all pupils of Hubay[1] and played in the same way. My three years in Budapest were very fruitful. I conducted an extraordinary number of concerts, and at the opera I did all the five main Mozart operas, *Tannhäuser*, *Lohengrin*, *Meistersinger*, *Fidelio*, *Rosenkavalier*, *Otello*, *Traviata*, *Hoffman* and a really unimportant work by Mussorgsky, *Sorotchintsy Fair*.

HEYWORTH: What was the singing like?

KLEMPERER: Very good. Budapest had some extraordinary voices at that time. The only trouble was that they only sang in Hungarian. Very stupid. At first there wasn't the slightest political pressure. Toth himself wasn't a Communist and refused to join the party. He did everything in his power to make life agreeable for me. I have never had a director who had more feeling for art or human understanding. He was dismissed during the 1956 uprising, something I wholeheartedly regret.

HEYWORTH: In what way did they finally fail to make life agreeable for you?

KLEMPERER: In my third year the influence of politics began to become impossible. The Hungarians wanted to stand well with the Russians—they were more or less under Russian rule. Whenever I needed the stage, a Soviet choreographer was having rehearsals for *The Nutcracker*. It was only with difficulty that I was able to hold my rehearsals for a new production of *La Traviata*. Then I wanted to do Schoenberg's *Theme and Variations* Opus 43b. Not the Opus 31 Variations; it isn't dodecaphonic, there's nothing revolutionary about it. I sent the score to the Minister of Culture, and he returned it, saying that he couldn't allow it, it wasn't socialist realism, no one would understand it and what was needed was music people could understand and love. So I didn't return from a tour I had in Australia.

HEYWORTH: You haven't been back to eastern Europe since?

KLEMPERER: For a long time I wasn't invited. And later, when Gilels and Oistrakh

[1] Jenö Hubay (1858–1937). Hungarian violinist and composer. Professor of the violin at the Budapest Conservatory.

a   Los Angeles about 1936

b   Bust by Anna Mahler, standing in the new hall of the Los Angeles Philharmonic, about 1946

c   With Arnold Schoenberg and Ernst Toch (*on the right*), Los Angeles, 1936

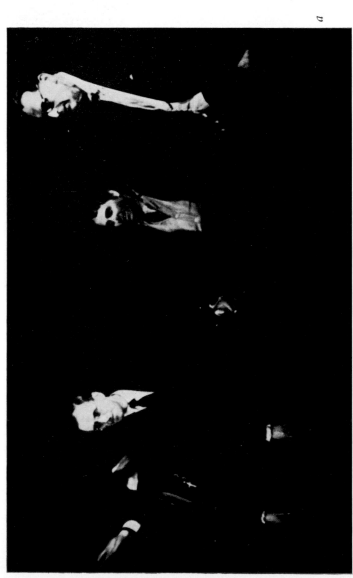

a With Walter Felsenstein (*left*), taking a curtain call after *Carmen* at the Komische Oper, East Berlin in 1948

b Conducting in Sydney, 1 October 1950

c Leaving Budapest, 1950

wanted me to go to Russia, it had become difficult for me. Look, the Soviet Union is one of Israel's main enemies. It helps Egypt, it has sent troops and the Mediterranean is full of Russian ships. I couldn't go. And it's the same with Prague and Budapest, which I would have liked to return to. All these Warsaw Pact countries make common cause against Israel. I can't work there on that basis. I don't want Israel to go down. On the contrary.

HEYWORTH: Are there no recordings of your opera performances in Budapest?

KLEMPERER: For a long while, I thought not. But recently recordings of *Die Meistersinger*, *Fidelio* and *The Tales of Hoffman*, all in Hungarian, have been discovered.

HEYWORTH: Didn't you also in this period conduct *Carmen* in a production by Felsenstein at the Komische Oper in East Berlin?

KLEMPERER: Yes, that was in 1948. The first thing I saw in his theatre was *Orpheus in the Underworld*. That was enchanting and very amusing, and as I had conducted it myself, it pleased me especially. Then I heard that he was going to do *Carmen*. I asked him whether he had engaged a conductor and suggested myself. The first night was put off many times, because the production wasn't as Felsenstein and I wanted. But finally it was a gigantic success. It gave me a lot of pleasure. Felsenstein really is a producer of genius. Only one must control him, otherwise he carries things to excess and does too much. The Michaela and the José were excellent, but the Carmen wasn't good at all.

HEYWORTH: How did you support the month-long rehearsals?

KLEMPERER: I enjoyed them. They lasted about three months, not more. Sometimes Felsenstein takes up to nine months on a production, and then at the last rehearsal he says that it doesn't please him and that he's going to do another work. But the régime always supports him. That's really extraordinary, the way they back him up. Very good.

HEYWORTH: And after Budapest?

KLEMPERER: I travelled around. I was in Buenos Aires, Australia and then in Montreal, where at the airport in autumn 1951 I fell and broke my hip. I had to go into hospital in Canada for eight months. It wasn't until 1955 that I was again able to conduct standing. In the winter of 1952 I was finally well enough to be able to arrange a tour in Europe for 1953. But then the Americans refused to renew our passports on account of the McCarren/Walter bill[1] and for a year I was virtually a prisoner. I had to cancel all my European engagements and it was far too late to get new ones in America for that season.

Eventually I found a good lawyer and in 1954 he got us temporary passports valid for six months. After various engagements we went to Switzerland. Where else could we have gone? My wife wanted to live in a German-speaking country—

[1] This put a limit on the time naturalised American citizens could remain outside the United States within a given period. The supreme Court has since declared it unconstitutional.

F

she was no linguist. Germany—no; and not Austria. So that summer we settled in Zürich. I have lived there ever since. I took a German passport and have worked mainly in London.

HEYWORTH: How did your connections with London come about?

KLEMPERER: I first came in 1929, when I conducted Bruckner's Eighth Symphony and Schoenberg's instrumentation of the Bach E flat prelude and fugue at a Courtauld–Sargent concert.[1] The orchestra was very bad. Schnabel, with whom I was good friends, had told Mrs Courtauld that she should invite me, but that I must have sufficient rehearsals. But the orchestra was as bad in the fifth rehearsal as it had been in the first. On the evening the trumpeters in the Bach–Schoenberg fugue were strange. I spoke to Sargent and asked him why they had been changed. "Oh," he said, "I thought it better not to tell you before the performance, because you might have been too upset." It was impossible. The following year things were much better and I conducted Beethoven's Ninth Symphony. It was well prepared, the chorus was good and the orchestra seemed a little better.

HEYWORTH: In this respect things have improved in London?

KLEMPERER: Not only the music, but also the food. It used to be terrible. I remember that I also conducted some Hindemith.[2] But I felt that Bruckner was not good for the audience's artistic digestion. It didn't like it. Then I went to America, and the next time I came to London was for the Festival of Britain in 1951. Then I was engaged with Schnabel. But he couldn't come, because he was too ill—it was only a few months before his death. And so in the first concert Dame Myra Hess played Beethoven's Emperor Concerto, really wonderfully. I was pleased to see that she used music, because it is vanity to suppose you can memorise everything. Memory is not important. I am sad that I never had another chance to perform with her.

In the second Festival of Britain concert I discovered that I was supposed to do Elgar's *Enigma Variations* as well as Walton's *Scapino* overture. But why should I do the Elgar when I was already doing the Walton, who is also a British composer? Why couldn't I do the Jupiter Symphony? "Impossible, impossible. We can't change the programme; they specially want to hear the *Enigma Variations* done by a foreign conductor." "In that case I shall not conduct." Then they changed their minds. And so I conducted the Jupiter Symphony.

Walter Legge[3] came to that concert, because it was his orchestra, the Philharmonia, that was playing. He liked the Jupiter Symphony and especially the last movement. After the concert he invited my wife and myself to have dinner at his house, and he talked without stopping until three or four o'clock in the morning.

[1] In 1929 Sir (then Dr) Malcolm Sargent (1895–1967) collaborated with Mrs Samuel Courtauld, in founding an annual series of concerts at the Queen's Hall.
[2] *Kammermusik No. 2* (Piano Concerto), Opus 36, no 1.
[3] 1906– . Artistic director of Columbia Records and founder of the Philharmonia Orchestra.

Legge is an able man. He has a very strong personality and expresses himself forcefully. For instance, he said, "Do you know why they closed the Kroll Opera? You went too far, you did too many modern things. You were wrong." My goodness! Meanwhile my wife slept on the sofa. But the first words I said to her after we left were, "That is a very dangerous man. He knows a lot, yes. But he is dangerous."

A few weeks later a letter arrived asking me to conduct his orchestra and make records with it, and suggesting that we meet in Salzburg to discuss details. We did so, but at that time nothing came of it. Then, as I've already told you, I was ill and lost my passport and couldn't come to Europe until 1954. At that time I was inwardly very undecided whether to go back to America or to stay in Europe. We had dinner with Legge in Milan and he said, "Stay in Europe. I can guarantee you a certain income through recordings." So it was decided and next winter I came to London to conduct the Philharmonia.

HEYWORTH: At that time there was no question of you becoming chief conductor?

KLEMPERER: No, no. Karajan was chief conductor at that time. I made many, many recordings of almost the whole classical repertory. Then Legge announced that he was also going to create a chorus[1] under Herr Pitz, who came every week from Aachen to rehearse. The first time it appeared in public was in Beethoven's Ninth Symphony in the first Beethoven cycle[2] I gave in London, in 1957, and it well deserved the enthusiastic reception it got. Arrau played all the piano concertos.

HEYWORTH: Did you find you could perform what you wanted?

KLEMPERER: Within the limitations of the box office. For instance, I wanted very much to do Bruckner's Sixth Symphony. But it's not popular and Legge always said, "Not now."[3]

HEYWORTH: But you found the conditions of working in London better than they had been before the war?

KLEMPERER: Much better. First I made the recording—for that one wants time—and only then did I give a concert performance. It all went quite well, and in 1959 Legge offered me a lifelong contract. It is amusing to think that I accepted it, but that Legge didn't make a lifelong contract with the orchestra.

HEYWORTH: What happened?

KLEMPERER: The events were highly unpleasant. In March 1964, out of the blue, Legge summoned the orchestral committee and told them that he was resigning. His secretary telephoned Lotte and said that Mr Legge had decided to dissolve the

[1] The Philharmonia Chorus.
[2] Klemperer conducted further Beethoven cycles in London in 1959 and 1970, shortly after his eighty-fifth birthday, and also in Vienna in 1960.
[3] Klemperer eventually recorded Bruckner's Sixth Symphony with the New Philharmonia Orchestra after Legge's retirement.

orchestra. But two players, Mr Morris and Mr Walton came to see me on its behalf to ask if I would become its president and continue to conduct it. I said yes, and I haven't regretted it.

I can only say that the New Philharmonia Orchestra has always given me the greatest pleasure, not only because it plays well, but because it has always behaved decently, which is something one can't say for all orchestras. But in January 1972 I thought that the time had come to retire from public concert-giving. However, I still intend to make occasional recordings and I remain the orchestra's president.

HEYWORTH: What about Covent Garden? How did it come about that that is the only theatre in which you have conducted opera since you left Budapest?[1]

KLEMPERER: Wieland Wagner and I planned to do *Tristan und Isolde* at the Holland Festival in 1959. Unfortunately in October 1958 I suffered third degree burns and was unable to work for a year. I made several premature attempts to start again, but it was no good. Then we finally began rehearsals, but to my very great regret I had to give up. We also had plans for Bayreuth. We had decided to do *Die Meistersinger*. We even discussed the cast and I was looking forward to it. But my health kept playing me damnable tricks. He also wanted me to conduct the Ninth Symphony for some sort of jubilee at Bayreuth. He asked me to come with the Philharmonia Orchestra and I gladly accepted. But then there were difficulties. The festival orchestra wanted to play and I wanted to come with the Londoners. So nothing came of it.

I found Wieland Wagner really agreeable and refreshing. But he was very ready to make concessions. I said to him, "Why have you cut some of the choruses in the second act in your production of *Lohengrin*?" "Because I don't like them." Well, I don't like them either, but I said to him, "Now listen, if I were to conduct *Lohengrin* with you I would do the choruses." "Of course," he said, "please do."

He was nice, but too conciliatory. I don't mean that he should have stuck to his ideas, as a faithful dog follows his master. But it's very important to have the capacity to say no. In New York in 1941 I refused to conduct *Siegfried Idyll* because they wanted it with full orchestra. I told them it was a chamber work with single woodwind and strings. They wouldn't agree, so I said, "Well you can do it without me.[2] Good-bye."

Then later in the sixties Sellner wanted me to do *Die Meistersinger* at the Deutsche Oper in West Berlin. But by then I was afraid of the long third act. I didn't dare, because sitting for two hours would have been too much for me. I was also invited by Rudolf Bing to conduct *Tristan* at the Met. in the season of 1959–1960. But my health rebelled again. I couldn't do it and he never asked me again.

[1] In fact Klemperer conducted *Die Zauberflöte* at La Scala, Milan in 1950 and *Fidelio* in Zürich in 1961.
[2] In German less polite. "Na, haben Sie mich mal gern."

a

a Covent Garden rehearsal for *Fidelio*,
18 February 1961 (*photo* Dominic)

b Covent Garden rehearsal for *Fidelio*,
26 February 1969 (*photo* Dominic)

b

a

b

c

a Drawing by Willy Dreifuss, Zürich, 1960
b With his grandson, Mark, Zürich, 1966
c Bust by Nigel Konstam, 1967 (*photo* Martin Breese)
d With Boulez in the Royal Festival Hall during a rehearsal of Stockhausen's *Gruppen*, February 1968
(*photo* G. Macdomnic)

d

The suggestion that I should conduct and produce[1] *Fidelio* at Covent Garden originally came in 1958 or 1959. I said, "What about the sets?" They sent me models and I found them awful. I said, "No, I want new sets." Webster[2] very honestly said, "I cannot do that this year; my budget doesn't allow it. But I promise that the moment I can, I will." And a year and a half later he came with Harewood[3] and we decided everything, that Jurinac should sing *Fidelio* and so on.

HEYWORTH: But when you did *Fidelio* at Covent Garden in 1961 it was not stylised in the manner of Wieland Wagner. Have you changed your mind about this?

KLEMPERER: Perhaps, a little. Yes. When I conducted at Covent Garden I tried to show a different aspect of *Fidelio* to what I had shown in Berlin.

HEYWORTH: At Covent Garden you conducted *Leonore No. 3* before the finale and at the Kroll you didn't.

KLEMPERER: The old question. In Berlin I felt that the drama is finished in the dungeon scene and now comes the finale. Today I don't think that that is right. The drama is finished—yes. But then Beethoven raises this story of an individual, who lives in chains and is rescued by a loving woman, to a universal level. The destiny of the individual becomes the destiny of the human race. It is no longer a matter of Florestan's fate but of Beethoven's outlook. He repeats the whole story in the overture and I think this repetition gives added meaning to the performance as a whole. At any rate, that's my opinion today. I can't tell you what it will be tomorrow!

HEYWORTH: In London you also produced *Fidelio*.

KLEMPERER: The reason why I decided to produce *Fidelio* and *Die Zauberflöte* at Covent Garden was to make sure that the musical conception shouldn't be disturbed by what happened on the stage. I think one must hold fast to Mozart's famous words: the text should always be the obedient daughter of the music. That says everything. During my whole life I've had a certain struggle with producers, because I didn't want the music to be interfered with. That's why I also sometimes produced at the Kroll Opera and elsewhere. A conductor should in any case be concerned with the performances of individual artists. Perhaps it's just a matter of ability whether he also takes responsibility for the whole stage but of course one needs a lot of time.

[1] A suggestion that no doubt partly originated from Dr Klemperer.
[2] Sir David Webster 1903–1971. General Administrator of Covent Garden 1945–1971.
[3] The Earl of Harewood 1923–. At that time on the staff of Covent Garden. Managing director of Sadlers Wells Opera since 1972.

CHAPTER VI

Conductors and Conducting

HEYWORTH: Dr Klemperer, what is the art of conducting?

KLEMPERER: The art of conducting lies, in my opinion, in the power of suggestion that the conductor exerts—on the audience as well as on the orchestra. A conductor must know how to hold attention. He must be able to lead the players with his eyes and the movements of his hands or baton. By this power of suggestion the level of a mediocre orchestra can be raised considerably. Vice versa, the playing art of a great orchestra can be lowered by a mediocre conductor.

HEYWORTH: Can one teach this art?

KLEMPERER: What one can teach and what one can learn is so minimal that I could explain it to you in a minute: for instance, how one beats 4/4, 3/4 and 5/8. These are externals. One must also learn to give special attention to the upbeats. And the second note must sometimes be a bit shorter than the first; that's something you can't notate. But the important thing is that one should let the orchestra breathe. That's the essential thing.

HEYWORTH: One of the characteristics of your performances seems to me to be a certain openness of sound and the prominence of the woodwind.

KLEMPERER: There you are right. It is most important that one should hear the woodwind, and generally you can't because the brass and the strings are too loud. I have always given special attention to the woodwind.

HEYWORTH: How do you get your particular sort of rhythmic articulation?

KLEMPERER: I don't know whether such a thing as personal rhythmic articulation exists. But I can tell you this: the conductor's hand delineates the music as far as possible, and most important of all is that the rhythmic articulation should give the players a chance to breathe. That isn't given enough attention by some conductors.

HEYWORTH: Could I ask you to say something about your conception of a right tempo?

KLEMPERER: One feels it. I mean, it was characteristic of Mahler's conducting that one felt that the tempo could not be otherwise.

HEYWORTH: Do you think your own tempi have become slower?

KLEMPERER: No, I don't feel that they have. I know people say that they're now too slow. But I don't think they are slower than they were.

HEYWORTH: Well, your Vox recording of Bruckner Four . . .

KLEMPERER: Oh, that was made a long time ago.

HEYWORTH: Just so. And the tempi are faster than in your more recent recording.

KLEMPERER: But that I made with the Philharmonia and it is better.

HEYWORTH: Maybe. But the tempi are broader.

KLEMPERER: Oh, are they?

HEYWORTH: Do you think that one tempo can be right for one performance and another tempo right for a different performance?

KLEMPERER: It could be, yes. But generally one sticks to the same tempo.

HEYWORTH: Can you explain how a conductor is able to realise his own particular sound? For instance, when *you* conduct there is invariably an absolutely individual quality of sound, irrespective of which orchestra you are conducting.

KLEMPERER: It's a very mysterious thing. When I conducted the Berlin Philharmonic a few years ago in a performance of Beethoven's Fourth, Stresemann, the Intendant, told me that the orchestra had just played the work under Karajan and that it had been completely different in every respect. I can perhaps say a few words. Very important is the upbeat; it's the upbeat and not the downbeat that makes an orchestra attentive. Then the first beat always has a certain weight and there I learnt much from Brecher.[1] One of the most important points is, I believe, that the conductor's hand should give the musicians the opportunity to play as though they were quite free. The players are hindered when the conductor beats too emphatically. For instance, in *fortissimo* entries the conductor shouldn't emphasise the entry enormously. The orchestra must do it. *They* must play. The conductor can only indicate *how* they should play.

HEYWORTH: But that particular sound? Can that be explained?

KLEMPERER: No. It's impossible to explain, at any rate more than I've done. It depends of course on the hand.

HEYWORTH: When did you give up using a baton?

KLEMPERER: After my operation in 1939. My right side was a little weak. It still is, but it is stronger than it was and a few years ago[2] I started to conduct again with a stick, because I feel it is more precise. Now I use a stick. But perhaps tomorrow I won't.

HEYWORTH: I read somewhere that you had given up using a baton before your operation.

KLEMPERER: Oh, no, no. And I never sat before the operation. Today I have to.

HEYWORTH: Do you find that the style of an individual orchestra, such as that of, say,

[1] See p. 39.   [2] 1967.

the Vienna Philharmonic as opposed to the Philadelphia Orchestra, affects your own performance?

KLEMPERER: Yes. I think that the Vienna Philharmonic is much better than all the American orchestras, though there are lots of European players in them and when someone like Toscanini conducts them they can be fabulously good. I also prefer the Vienna orchestra to the Berlin Philharmonic. But individual members can be very disagreeable. They're not easy to handle. But it's wonderful how they can play—especially the strings. I last conducted them in 1968. The Bruckner Fifth was splendid, the Mahler Ninth not so good. But there were special reasons for that. The Mahler hadn't been performed in Vienna for a long time. One critic wrote, "One could note that the spirit that drove Mahler out of Vienna is in no way only historical."

HEYWORTH: You yourself had an impression that the orchestra was resistent to the music?

KLEMPERER: Yes, yes. But, oh my goodness, I like Vienna. Maybe it is an unhappy love, but I love it. I know the people are false, always very complimentary—though not behind one's back.

I must tell you a story. Senator Robert Kennedy was assassinated[1] just before that concert in which I was to conduct Mahler's Ninth, and I said that we would open it with Mozart's *Masonic Funeral Music*. Then the orchestral committee approached Lotte.[2] When there is something disagreeable they always come to Lotte, and never to me. They asked, "Who made this decision to play the *Masonic Funeral Music*?"

"My father."

"Oh, but, you see, it is political."[3]

"Political?"

So I had an announcement put in the programme that it was played in memory of the murdered senator at the special wish of the conductor. Then the director of the Musikverein, Gamsjäger, said, "Look, this word 'murdered' in the programme is so ugly. Could we not just say 'In Memoriam?'" I agreed.

That's Vienna for you. But, you see, the surroundings—the Semmering, Grinzing—are wonderful. There is music, the greatest music, in the stones of the streets. I love it.

HEYWORTH: You said that the conductor also influences the audience. Can you explain that?

[1] 6 June 1968.
[2] Klemperer's daughter, who has accompanied her father on his conducting engagements, especially since the death of his wife in 1956.
[3] The Vienna Philharmonic was shortly to embark on a tour of the United States and was no doubt anxious to avoid anything that might be interpreted as involvement in American politics.

KLEMPERER: It depends on the conductor's personality, and everything contributes to that, even the visual. Nikisch, for instance, was an absolute beau. He had wonderful hands and always showed a lot of cuff—the black of his evening dress and the white of his cuffs was tremendously effective. There's a lot of acting in conducting.

But there is a distinction I would very much like to make between conductors who also compose and conductors who just conduct, and Nikisch was an example of a conductor who didn't compose. He was really a virtuoso. Strauss thought a lot of him. But I think he was a better conductor than he was a musician. He conducted the Schumann symphonies wonderfully, and also Wagner and Strauss. His parade pieces were the *Tannhäuser* overture and, above all, Tchaikovsky's *Symphonie Pathétique*, which he did phenomenally—great beauty of sound, controlled and yet very passionate. No, he was wonderful.

He also conducted at the Hamburg Opera while I was there. I remember a *Fledermaus* that he conducted with immense charm. And also *The Ring*. He was a professional charmer. When he first appeared before an orchestra, he would greet a player, whom he had probably never seen before, "Ah, *grüss Gott*, dear friend, and how are you? We haven't seen each other for so long." The whole orchestra would laugh. He used to play poker throughout the night. But it didn't seem to do him any harm.

He used to conduct Mahler, though he didn't really like his music. Both of them had been together at the Leipzig opera and before long they had become rivals.[1] Nikisch had quite a different approach to music from Mahler. He always said, "I can only conduct if I feel the music in my heart." But I think that was true. He had a very romantic attitude. But then you see, the difference between Strauss and Mahler on the one hand and Nikisch on the other was that Strauss and Mahler were composers, whereas Nikisch was just a conductor—a very good conductor.

HEYWORTH: What did you feel about Toscanini?

KLEMPERER: A splendid conductor with a phenomenal sense of sound and memory, and yet basically naïve in the best sense of the word—though he didn't compose either. He was a man who knew exactly what he wanted and how to get it. I couldn't always agree with *what* he wanted, but I admired him very much. I went to his rehearsals and how he achieved that special sound was a miracle. I couldn't see that it had anything to do with any of his gestures. I heard many of his concerts. Haydn's Clock Symphony—wonderful, wonderful. About the same time he also conducted some Respighi—I think it is called *The Pines of Rome*. For me, it is a terrible piece, but his performance was amazing. And his Wagner was very, very good. I heard him conduct *Die Meistersinger* in Milan. Excellent, excellent.

HEYWORTH: Did you ever feel that his tempi were too fast?

[1] Nikisch was first conductor in Leipzig from 1879 to 1889, Mahler an assistant conductor from 1886–1888. Mahler left for Budapest largely on account of tension between him and his superior.

KLEMPERER: Yes, much too fast. Beethoven's First Symphony was excellent—clear and quite unromantic. But in, for instance, the Seventh he took the trio much too fast. So far as I know, it's an old Austrian pilgrims' song, an Ave Maria. He didn't understand that. It only makes sense when it is taken slowly. It should be a contrast to the scherzo.

And then he had this mania for conducting by heart, without the music. It wasn't that he was blind; he was short-sighted, but he was too vain to wear glasses. If he had done so, he would have been able to read scores. I think it's foolish to conduct without the music. I did it myself for years. When I did the Lulu Suite[1] in New York, I told Judson that I would have to have a week off to learn it. I got a week's leave, but it wouldn't have been necessary if I had conducted with the music.

HEYWORTH: But doesn't one get to know a piece better in the process of learning it by heart?

KLEMPERER: Yes. But for many conductors it means little more than counting. They may beat it correctly, but they don't listen to the music. I heard Blech's son-in-law[2] conduct a very complicated and difficult ballet in Sweden without a score and afterwards I asked him about it.

"Tell me, how do you learn a work like that? Can you play it at the piano?"
"Impossible."
"Have you often heard it performed by an orchestra?"
"No."
"Well, you can't know what they are playing."
"I don't."
"Well, for goodness sake, in that case you have absolutely no control. The orchestra could play 'Deutschland, Deutschland über alles' without you noticing it."

That's the madness of conducting without a score. I think that anyone who feels more secure with the music should use it. And anyone who feels happier without it, should do without it. It's a matter of taste. The important thing is to know the work inwardly.[3]

HEYWORTH: Do you think that conducting without music hindered Toscanini?

KLEMPERER: Finally, I think it did. A friend, who saw him in his room before a performance of *Falstaff* at Salzburg, told me that he paced up and down, saying, "If only I don't make a mistake."

HEYWORTH: But his Verdi was wonderful, wasn't it?

[1] Suite made by Berg from his opera, *Lulu*.
[2] Herbert Ludwig Sandberg (1902–66). Swedish conductor of German origin.
[3] A pun, impossible to reproduce in English. To learn inwardly is "inwendig lernen"; to learn by heart is "auswendig lernen".

KLEMPERER: Wonderful. In 1929 he brought the Scala singers[1] and orchestra—to Berlin and conducted unforgettable performances of *Il Trovatore* and *Falstaff*, and also of *Lucia di Lammermoor*.

HEYWORTH: What about Mengelberg?

KLEMPERER: He was a very good trainer, and the Concertgebouw is his creation. He was excellent in pieces like Tchaikovsky's Fifth Symphony. And he gave an entire Mahler festival in 1920—he had been a great friend of Mahler in his lifetime.

HEYWORTH: Did he have a very distinctive style of performing him?

KLEMPERER: No. Mengelberg was an excellent trainer rather than a great conductor. He knew how to master an orchestra and he had very good ears. Unfortunately he did a lot of silly things during the war. He is said to have sent Hitler a telegram of congratulations after his entry into Paris. As a result he was not allowed to conduct after the war and he died in Switzerland. I conducted the memorial concert for him in Amsterdam.

HEYWORTH: We haven't talked about Furtwängler, except for the attempt to appoint him as Toscanini's successor in New York.

KLEMPERER: I used to see Furtwängler in Munich before the First World War. He always went there at vacation time, and we used to go for walks together. One day he played me his tempi for a Beethoven symphony. They were very good and I felt that here was a born musician. And later on he reached the top as conductor of both the Gewandhaus[2] Orchestra and of the Berlin Philharmonic.[3] It was in Berlin that he gave the first performance of Schoenberg's *Orchestral Variations*, Opus 31.[4]

HEYWORTH: Did you hear that?

KLEMPERER: Yes, I did. It was a very good performance. But the audience didn't like it at all. There was a terrible scandal. A few people applauded, but most of the audience whistled and then, when the orchestra took a bow, there was enormous applause. I asked Schoenberg, "Why weren't you there? You should have heard it." He replied, "I don't like hearing my music booed." But he appeared to be very satisfied with the rehearsals. It speaks for Furtwängler that he did the work.

I very much admired the power of suggestion he exercised, on the public as well as the orchestra. But he did some curious things. For instance, I heard him conduct Bach's *Suite in B minor* in Berlin before 1933. The coda to the first movement is, I find, a wonderful synthesis, and he left it out. Cut it out. At the concert I talked to Hindemith and asked him what he thought of it. "Oh," he said, "Furtwängler doesn't understand Bach at all."

[1] Of Milan.

[2] Leipzig orchestra, traditionally one of Germany's greatest.

[3] Furtwängler was appointed conductor of both orchestras in 1922 as Nikisch's successor.

[4] 1928.

But some things he understood very well. I remember particularly how he conducted Tchaikovsky's Fifth Symphony with passionate temperament, just before I left Berlin in 1933. I had to think of Wagner's words, "Is that German?" That he should have been so interested in Tchaikovsky was incomprehensible to me. That was the last time I saw him. I never met or heard him after the war.

HEYWORTH: Did you hear him conduct Wagner?

KLEMPERER: Yes, I heard him do *Die Meistersinger* in Berlin. When there was a symphonic piece for the orchestra alone, it was very good. But when there were singers, it was not so good. He was no opera conductor. He would be angry if he heard me say so, but I think he was absolutely a concert conductor.

HEYWORTH: Am I right in thinking that he specialised in subtle variations of tempo?

KLEMPERER: Yes, his rubato was very well measured, not too much and not too little.

HEYWORTH: What do you think of Stokowski?

KLEMPERER: A lot. I recently heard him on television. He is better than he was. In the past he was a bit too free in questions of style. He made those terrible arrangements, like the Bach *Toccata and Fugue in D minor*. But everything he conducts sounds well.

HEYWORTH: How do you think he gets that sound?

KLEMPERER: He never makes enormous gestures, but the orchestra feels it has to be attentive and the strings play with vibrato. He has a personal influence on the orchestra. The Philadelphia Orchestra under Stokowski was really a giant. As it was, that is, not as it is now; at that time it was really overwhelming. Then he went to Hollywood, where he made hair-raisingly bad films, one worse than the other.

HEYWORTH: What about the younger generation of conductors? Karajan, for instance?

KLEMPERER: Karajan is an extremely talented conductor. I heard, for instance, a performance of *Falstaff* with Italian singers in Vienna. It was really excellent. But I heard the Ninth Symphony in Lucerne, and that was terrible. After the scherzo I left the hall.

HEYWORTH: Why?

KLEMPERER: It was too quick, much too quick. And in the Ninth Symphony Beethoven's metronome markings are good. In the scherzo it is 116 to the whole bar—no quicker.

I also heard Karajan once in Amsterdam. He conducted Bruckner's Seventh very well. But, you see, at the Concertgebouw the entrance for the conductor is a long way from the rostrum; he has to walk down a long stairway, and to see how Karajan came back to take applause, with open arms and bows to all sides, that was a piece of theatre. It was comic. I couldn't see that it was necessary for him to put on this show. He is a good man, he can conduct, and that's that. I don't understand why he is so addicted to applause. But he has a very nice wife, that I

a Leaving his 85th birthday concert on 14 May 1970 (*photo* G. Macdomnic)

b Receiving a birthday cake at a rehearsal on his 86th birthday, 14 May 1971 (*photo* G. Macdomnic)

   With Ernst Bloch, 1968

d With Paul Dessau, 1968

e Reading, 1968

a

b

c

d

e

Zürich, November 1972
Lotte Klemperer appears below

must say—a charming girl from Paris. He's just the conductor for 1969.[1]

HEYWORTH: Would you rate Boulez highly as a conductor?

KLEMPERER: Yes, very highly. He is without doubt the only man of his generation who is an outstanding conductor *and* musician. I'm not speaking now of how he conducts his own works, but other music. I've heard him conduct Haydn, Mozart, Schumann, Wagner, Debussy and Stravinsky, and also Stockhausen's *Gruppen*, which was magnificent, wasn't it? Without doubt he is a man of his time in the best sense of the word. He may have his weaknesses and limitations, but what I've heard has been excellent.

HEYWORTH: Would you say that the creative element also plays a role here?

KLEMPERER: And how! But some of his views on music are very strange. For example, Lotte and I had dinner with him at his London hotel. He said he didn't like Italian music.

"You don't like *Falstaff*?"

"No."

"And *Otello*?"

"No."

"Absolutely nothing? No Italian music at all? The Verdi *Requiem*?"

"No."

I couldn't understand it. I stood before an enigma. Perhaps you can explain it?

HEYWORTH: I suspect that fifteen years ago he might have said the same thing about Wagner. It sometimes seems to me that he is making a journey of discovery into the past and recovering territory he had previously rejected.

But it's very depressing. You say that in your opinion Boulez stands alone among his generation. Yet if one looks at that photograph taken when Toscanini came to Berlin in 1929, there is Walter, Furtwängler, Kleiber and yourself.[2] One may value them differently, but nonetheless there was at that time a great generation of conductors. Do you think that there has since been a decline in the general level of conducting?

KLEMPERER: A big decline. People are always telling me, "Oh, I heard the Seventh Symphony conducted by so-and-so and it was wonderful." I say, "You must not tell me such things. I have heard the same symphony conducted by Mahler and I know." The integrity is lacking. I don't want to mention names, but a few years ago in Salzburg there was a concert by a young conductor. Everyone said what enormous talent he had and so forth. So I went to his final rehearsal. He did Beethoven's Eighth Symphony with the Berlin Philharmonic, who can really play a Beethoven symphony from start to finish without a conductor. The performance

---

[1] The year in which these conversations took place.

[2] Walter, Kleiber and Klemperer were the musical directors of Berlin's three opera houses, Furtwängler of the Berlin Philharmonic Orchestra. The picture faces p. 65.

was very, very bad. Afterwards the conductor came over to me and expected me to say that I'd never before heard it played so beautifully. I asked him, "When is the performance?"

"This evening."

"This evening! Are you going to play it like that?"

"Oh, don't worry. In the evening the orchestra will play like angels. They are just a little sloppy in rehearsals."

"But that is the first and last rehearsal?"

"Yes."

In the programme he had, I think, Bartók's *Concerto for Orchestra* and Strauss's *Four Last Songs*, and he had rehearsed both scores enormously; but the Beethoven not at all, although it's certainly the most difficult.

The trouble with this younger generation is that they forget the steps. One cannot begin with *Wozzeck* and end with a Haydn symphony. One must begin with Haydn, go on to Mozart, Beethoven and Schubert and then one may be able to move on to more recent and more complicated music. Don't you agree? The trouble is that they have no sense of maturing: they want to get to the top right away. That is very bad for their development. I tell you that if I were to have to suggest a permanent conductor for the New Philharmonia Orchestra, I wouldn't know who to name. The mediocrities, they are the emperors today.

HEYWORTH: Do you think that the conditions in which conductors are now more or less obliged to function play a part in this decline of standards?

KLEMPERER: Yes, a big part. Previously the conductor stayed with his job. Today there's too much temptation to travel. All this guest conducting is very unsatisfactory. After a few rehearsals everything is supposed to be ready for the concert. Yet the conductor doesn't know the orchestra and the orchestra doesn't know the conductor. And with quick travel comes the temptation to try to do too much.

In this I see a great danger for Boulez's future. I've more or less told him so. When we saw him recently[1] in Basle, Lotte said, "I congratulate you on your New York appointment." I said, "I offer you my condolences." I find it dreadful. He now has the New York Philharmonic, the BBC Symphony Orchestra and occasional obligations in Cleveland and elsewhere, and he composes. How can one man manage all that? What is important for him, in my opinion, is to develop as a composer. That he conducts splendidly; my goodness, that shouldn't be so terribly important for him.

HEYWORTH: Do you enjoy making gramophone records?

KLEMPERER: No, I hate it. I like to make a recording before a concert performance, because then I have time to prepare a work properly. But I hate this business of constantly moving to the control room to hear what I have recorded. I'm trying

[1] Boulez's appointment was announced in June 1969.

to free myself as far as possible from that. Toscanini's attitude is my ideal. I didn't experience it myself, but I'm told that he would agree, let us say, to record Beethoven's Seventh Symphony. But that was all. Afterwards he went home, and didn't stay to repeat two bars in the third movement or five in the finale. He refused to do that. I would like to do the same, or more or less the same.

HEYWORTH: Don't you want to hear a playback, so as to be able to say, "That I want to repeat" or "That I can improve on"?

KLEMPERER: I'm not much interested in that.

HEYWORTH: This preoccupation with detail and technical perfection irritates you?

KLEMPERER: Yes, of course. After all, music is a human thing. It isn't a disaster when a horn player gets a bit of saliva on his lips and the tone goes wrong. Good heavens, he is a human being. That's just the most important thing of all.

I would prefer to record a performance rather than to make a recording in a studio. A few mistakes don't matter. In any case, when I am recording I insist on playing at least overtures and whole movements without a break. I will not do eight bars and then another eight bars. I only do small stretches if I must. If, for instance, there is a wrong note in the horns and everything else is all right, then I agree. But now I stay on the rostrum and they can come and tell me what they want repeated. I'm not going to do the running around; they can.

HEYWORTH: Do you think that this habit some conductors have of recording a work in a series of tiny fragments destroys the sense of the music's form?

KLEMPERER: Completely, completely.

HEYWORTH: Do you think that recordings lead people to have a standardised view of a work, to suppose that the recording *is* the work?

KLEMPERER: Naturally that's a danger. But surely any moderately musical person must prefer a living performance to a gramophone record. Finally, a record is just a record. It can never be the same as a performance. But records bring music to places where nobody hears a great orchestra. They're not ideal; but they are better than nothing.

HEYWORTH: Are you satisfied with your own recordings?

KLEMPERER: As far as I know them, I am content.

HEYWORTH: You don't listen to your recordings or compare them to others?

KLEMPERER: No, no, no. Never. I don't like or dislike listening to them. I don't listen to them at all. With one exception, that is: I listen again and again to the Kyrie from the *B minor Mass*. That I love so much that I even enjoy listening to my own recording. It's a marvellous piece. And it isn't even original, in the sense that Bach had already used it in some other work.[1] One sees how free the whole notion of plagiarism was in the seventeenth and eighteenth centuries. Today, for

[1] Probably originally composed for a memorial service for the Elector Friedrich August I ("the strong") of Saxony.

heaven's sake, if three bars remind anyone of something else—plagiarism!

HEYWORTH: So, once your recordings are made, you are not much further concerned with them?

KLEMPERER: No. But I'm very interested whether they are sold or not!

HEYWORTH: What about music on TV?

KLEMPERER: I don't like it, the way the horns are shown, then a bit of the conductor, then the timpani. For me, that's unbearable. I also don't like the way rehearsals are televised. One should only show things *when* they are prepared, not *how* they are prepared. People enjoy seeing behind the scenes, but I don't like rehearsals in which I know that every movement and everything I say is recorded. No. The completed performance—that's what one must show. But music on television will have a future.

CHAPTER VII

The Conductor as Composer

HEYWORTH: When did you start to compose?

KLEMPERER: I started when I was very young. When I was about ten, my greatest pleasure was to put my school anthology on the piano and to improvise music to the poems. Then, later, about 1901, I started to compose songs.

HEYWORTH: What were the influences on your own music at this time?

KLEMPERER: When I went to Pfitzner in 1904 it was Brahms. I was much more enthusiastic about him than I was about Wagner. For me Brahms was the hero. At that time I wrote a concert overture. When I was trying to get a job as a conductor, I went to see Dr Muck,[1] and I played him this overture. He said that he would do it in Boston. Also my piano professor, James Kwast, said that he would play a piano trio I had written. But in both cases I didn't allow it, because I thought that the works were too much of an imitation of Brahms and not original enough. The trio was so like Brahms that it might have been mistaken for him. Not, of course, that I compare myself to Brahms, you understand, but I was so immersed in his harmony and melody that I couldn't write in any other way.

HEYWORTH: But later you started to compose music that you feel stands on its own feet stylistically?

KLEMPERER: Yes. That really began in Prague. It was there that I first heard Debussy's *Pelléas et Mélisande* in 1907. It made an enormous impression on me. It was a new world—the idea of a whole tone scale and all that. From that time I started to compose works which I would still stand up for today.

At first I composed songs—one of them was printed in a Christmas edition of *Bohemia*.[2] Then I composed the orchestral songs which I showed to Strauss,[3] and finally in 1915, when I was thirty, I composed two operas. One was called *Wehen*,

[1] Karl Muck (1859–1940). Famous Wagnerian, conductor of the Boston Symphony Orchestra 1906–1918.

[2] A Prague daily paper.

[3] See p. 41.

not 'Wehen' in the sense of the sound of the wind in the trees, but meaning labour pains. I wrote the text during my holidays, when I was staying with my parents in Hamburg, and I started on the score in a sanatorium where I had previously been with a bad depression in 1911. This time I was in a euphoric state and I thought that the sanatorium would have a quietening effect on me. That was a mistake. As soon as my sketches were complete I travelled to Munich to show them to my friend, Gustav Brecher.[1] He gave me good advice, and among much that was immature he saw a clear concept. But I never orchestrated it. Even today, I don't know why I didn't finish it.

The second opera is called *Das Ziel* and there I drew a little on the atmosphere of that sanatorium. People often go to a sanatorium because they are bored with life and sanatorium routine gives them something to do. *Das Ziel*[2] of the title is death. I mean, we humans don't know what the goal is. But we behave as though there is one. We go towards it, but we don't know where it lies. The goal is unknown, isn't it, yet we reach it. Look, all this borders on theological questions and we don't want to go into them. Anyway, the score lies peacefully in my desk. Whether it will ever be resurrected I cannot say. But the Merry Waltz from it has been recorded.

HEYWORTH: Is the fact that it has never been performed a disappointment to you?

KLEMPERER: No, no. Not a big disappointment. I'd be very happy if I could conduct it and hear how it goes. But eternity doesn't hang on it.

Later, in Strasbourg, I composed music for *Faust*, just the passages where Goethe asks for music—not a great Faust-cosmos. I performed it at a final concert of my own music that I gave there. But that was the only time. In 1919, the year I got married, I wrote a big *Missa Sacra* for six voices, orchestra and chorus. It's printed by Schott. And many, many songs. Heather Harper sang some of them at my seventy-fifth birthday party in London in 1960.

I've also written several operas on biblical texts. One of them is called *The Prodigal Son*. Another is *Juda*. But none of them has been done. Here and there people have shown interest, but . . . Now I wait patiently.

HEYWORTH: Are you more satisfied with your more recent music?

KLEMPERER: Yes, that is why I have rewritten some things. I don't think they were good in their original form. It's not for me to judge, but I think my Second Symphony is an advance on the First. The First was performed by Rosbaud in Baden-Baden and by Erede in Gothenburg and I have done it myself in London and Amsterdam. The Second I composed in 1967, and in 1969 I performed it in London. Like the First, it's published in London by Peters. EMI have issued a recording of it, with my Quartet No. 7 on the other side. Very nice!

I have written more symphonies. Now I am on No. 6. Sometimes I compose

[1] See p. 39.   [2] "The goal."

very quickly, too quickly. But it means I am always busy, and that is good.

HEYWORTH: What are the main influences on your mature compositions?

KLEMPERER: My God, naturally I have been influenced by Mahler. And also in a certain sense by Schoenberg; not by the second Viennese school, but by Schoenberg himself. Otherwise I don't know of anyone.

HEYWORTH: And the *neue Sachlichkeit*,[1] to use a slogan, were you drawn to that?

KLEMPERER: *Die neue Sachlichkeit*, understood as a reaction from a sentimental romanticism, had a certain influence on me.

HEYWORTH: May I ask you a question that I hope you won't find impertinent. Do you regard yourself as a conductor who happens to compose, or as a composer who has been unjustly neglected?[2]

KLEMPERER: It's a very difficult question. I can only say a few words. I am mainly a conductor who also composes. Naturally, I would be glad to be remembered as a conductor *and* as a composer. But, without wanting to be arrogant, I would only like to be remembered as a *good* composer. If people find my compositions weak, then it is better not to be remembered.

[1] "The new objectivity", used in Germany of the neo-classicism of the twenties, particularly in relation to Hindemith's music of that period.

[2] This is the only question of which Dr Klemperer asked notice; he replied to it at a later session.

Epilogue

HEYWORTH: Do you think there is a connection between great gifts and great suffering?

KLEMPERER (who does not welcome portentous questions and at first appeared not to hear this one, after a few minutes of general banter abruptly reached for his Bible, which is in Luther's translation, and read):

I have seen all the works that are done under the sun; and, behold, all is vanity and vexation of spirit.

That which is crooked cannot be made straight; and that which is wanting cannot be numbered.

I communed with mine own heart, saying, Lo, I am come to great estate, and have gotten more wisdom than all they that have been before me in Jerusalem: yea, my heart had great experience of wisdom and knowledge.

And I gave my heart to know wisdom, and to know madness and folly: I perceived that this also is vexation of spirit.

For in much wisdom is much grief; and he that increaseth knowledge increaseth grief.

(Ecclesiastes 1.14–18)

Discography and Index

Discography

compiled by Malcolm Walker

ABBREVIATIONS

A	Angel Records (USA)	H	His Master's Voice (UK)
Br	Brunswick (UK)	Fidelio	Delta (UK)
C	Columbia (UK)	P	Polydor (France and Germany)
Delta	Delta (UK)	V	Vox Productions (UK and USA)

New Philh. New Philharmonia Orchestra   Orch. Orchestra
Philh.   Philharmonia Orchestra

bs	bass	pf	piano
br	baritone	s	soprano
c	contralto	t	tenor
m-s	mezzo-soprano	vln	violin

PART ONE

78 rpm recordings made prior to 1933—all with the Berlin State Opera Orchestra
§ denotes pre-electrical recording made before 1928

AUBER. Fra Diavolo—Overture	P	E11201
BEETHOVEN. Symphony No. 1 in C major, Op. 21	P	66231–4§
BEETHOVEN. Symphony No. 8 in F major, Op. 93	P	66264–6
BEETHOVEN. Symphony No. 8 in F major, Op. 93	P	66339–41§
BEETHOVEN. Coriolan, Op. 62—Overture	P	66599
	D	CA8091
BEETHOVEN. Egmont, Op. 84—Overture	P	66600
BEETHOVEN. Leonore No. 3 Overture, Op. 72b	P	66601–2
BRAHMS. Symphony No. 1 in C minor, Op. 68	P	E10807–12

BRAHMS. Academic Festival Overture, Op. 80   H D1853–4
BRUCKNER. Symphony No. 8 in C minor—Adagio   P 66325–8§
DEBUSSY. Nocturnes—Nuages; Fêtes   P 66464–5
                                                             Br 80016–7
MENDELSSOHN. A Midsummer Night's Dream—Overture   P 66602–3
OFFENBACH. La belle Hélène—Overture   P E10935
RAVEL. Alborada del gracioso   P 66463
SCHUBERT. Symphony No. 8 in B minor, D759, "Unfinished"   P 66339–41
RICHARD STRAUSS. Don Juan   P E11051
RICHARD STRAUSS. Salome—Dance of the Seven Veils   H D1633
RICHARD STRAUSS. Till Eulenspiegel, Op. 28   P E10925–6
WAGNER. Siegfried Idyll   P 66604–5
WAGNER. Tristan und Isolde—prelude (with Wagner's concert ending) H E476–7
WEBER. Euryanthe—Overture   P 66629
WEILL. Kleine Dreigroschenmusik   P 24172–3
                                                            V 451

PART TWO

78 rpm and Microgroove recordings made since 1946 (between the years 1933 and 1946
Dr Klemperer made no commercial records)

RECORD CATEGORIES FOR LP DISCS

Index Letters	Numbers	Example	Type of Record
Roman Capitals	Roman	33CX1763	Mono 33⅓ rpm LP
Bold Face Capitals	Bold	**SAX 2408**	Stereo 33⅓ rpm LP
Italic lower case	Italic	*scd2178*	Mono 45 rpm SP
Italic Capitals	Italic	*SEL1677*	Mono 45 rpm EP
Bold Face lower case	Bold	**esl6283**	Stereo 45 rpm EP

Asterisk after number denotes 78 rpm records.

BACH
Brandenburg Concertos Nos. 1–6, BWV1046–51
   Paris Pro Musica Orch.   AmV 618–23*
   Nos. 1 & 2 / 3 & 4 / 5 & 6   VLP6180; 6200; 6220
      (NB. In this recording of Concerto No. 2 the
      trumpet part is played by saxophone and
      clarinet)
   Philh. (with George Malcolm, harpsichord)   C 33CX1763–4/**SAX2408–9**
                                                  A 3627B–L/**S–3627B–L**

Orchestral Suites Nos. 1–4, BWV1066–9
   Philh. (with Gareth Morris, flute)   C 33CX1239–40
                                                  A 3536BL

   New Philh. (with Gareth Morris, flute)   A **S–3627B**
                                                  H **SLS808**

Mass in B minor, BWV232
  with Agnes Giebel (s), Janet Baker (c), Nicolai
  Gedda (t), Hermann Prey (br), Franz Crass
  (bs), BBC Chorus, New Philh.   H **SAN195–7/SLS930**
                                                  A **S–3720C**

St Matthew Passion, BWV244—complete recording
  with Peter Pears (t), Dietrich Fischer-Dieskau
  (br), Walter Berry (bs), Elisabeth Schwarzkopf
  (s), Christa Ludwig (m–s), Nicolai Gedda (t),
  Hampstead Boys' Choir, Philh. Orch. &
  Chorus   C 33CXS1799, 33CX1800–3
                                                     /SAXS2446, SAX2447–50
                                                  H **SLS827**
                                                  A 3599E–L/**S–3599E–L**
Excerpts from complete recording   C 33CX1881/**SAX2525**
                                                  C 33CX5252/**SAX5252**
                                                  C *SEL1707*
                                                  A 36162–3/**S–36162–3**

BEETHOVEN
Symphonies—
  No. 1 in C major, Op. 21
  Philh./*Symphony No. 8*   C 33CX1554/**SAX2318**
                                                  A 35657/**S–35657**
                                                  H **ASD2560**

  No. 2 in D major, Op. 36
  Philh./*Coriolan and Prometheus Overtures*   C 33CX1615/**SAX2331**
                                                  A 35658/**S–35658**
      /Leonore No. 2 and Prometheus Overtures   H **ASD2561**
  No. 3 in E flat major, Op. 55, "Eroica"
  Philh.   C 33CX1346
                                                  A 35328

  Philh.   C 33CX1710/**SAX2364**
                                                  A 35853/**S–35853**
      /Fidelio Overture   H **ASD2562**
  No. 4 in B flat major, Op. 60
  Philh./*Consecration of the House Overture*   C 33CX1702/**SAX2354**
                                                  A 35661/**S–35561**
      /Egmont—incidental music   H **ASD2563**
  No. 5 in C minor, Op. 67
  Vienna Symphony Orch.   V PL7070
      /Mozart: not conducted by Klemperer   V PL11870
                                      Delta/Fidelio ATL4107
  Philh.   C 33C1051

/Consecration of the House Overture	A	35329
Philh./*King Stephen Overture*	C	33CX1721/**SAX2373**
	A	35843/**S–35843**
/Coriolan Overture	H	**ASD2564**
No. 6 in F major, Op. 68, "Pastoral"		
Vienna Symphony Orch.	V	PL6960
		GBY6960
Philh.	C	33CX1532/**SAX2260**
	A	35711/**S–35711**
/Leonore No. 1 Overture	H	**ASD2565**
No. 7 in A major, Op. 92		
Philh.	C	33CX1379
	A	35330
Philh.	C	33CX1869/**SAX2415**
	A	35945/**S–35945**
/Consecration of the House Overture	H	**ASD2566**
New Philh./*Rameau/Klemperer: Gavotte with Six*	H	**ASD2537**
Variations		
No. 8 in F major, Op. 93		
Philh./*Symphony No. 1*	C	33CX1554/**SAX2318**
	A	35657/**S–35657**
	H	**ASD2560**
No. 9 in D minor, Op. 125, "Choral"		
with Aase Nordmö-Lovberg (s), Christa Ludwig		
(m-s), Waldemar Kmentt (t), Hans Hotter		
(br), Philh. Orch. & Chorus (mono version		
coupled with *Egmont—incidental music*)	C	33CX1574–5/**SAX2276–7**
	A	3577B/**S–3577B**
/Leonore No. 3 and King Stephen Overtures	H	**ASD2567–8**
		SLS790

The Nine Symphonies were also issued in a nine-record boxed set on C and A 3619H/**S–3619H.**

To coincide with Dr Klemperer's eighty-fifth birthday in May 1970, EMI Records re-packaged all Nine Symphonies plus the Overtures—Leonore Nos. 1–3; Fidelio; Creatures of Prometheus; Coriolan; King Stephen; Consecration of the House; Egmont—incidental music, in a nine-record boxed set.   H   **SLS788**

Overtures—Coriolan; King Stephen; Consecration of the House; Creatures of Prometheus; Egmont Philh.   C   33CX1930/**SAX2570**

Overtures—Leonore Nos. 1, 2 & 3; Fidelio
    Philh.   C   33CX1270
                                         A   35258

    Philh.   C   33CX1902/**SAX2542**
                                         A   36209/**S36209**

Creatures of Prometheus, Op. 43—Overture and two
    excerpts
    New Philh.   H   To be released

Grosse Fuge, Op. 133 (orchestral version)
    Philh./*Mozart: Serenade No. 6; Adagio and Fugue*   C   33CX1438
                                           A   35401

Piano Concertos—
    No. 1 in C major, Op. 15
    No. 2 in B flat major, Op. 19
    No. 3 in C minor, Op. 37
    No. 4 in G major, Op. 58
    No. 5 in E flat major, Op. 73, "Emperor"
    Daniel Barenboim (pf), New Philh./*Choral*
    Fantasia   H   **SLS941**
                                           A   **S3752D–L**

    (Also issued individually as: No. 1: ASD2616;
    No. 2 & Choral Fantasia: ASD2608; No. 3:
    ASD2579; No. 4: ASD2550; No. 5: ASD
    2500)

No. 4 in G major, Op. 58
    Guiomar Novaes (pf), Vienna Symphony Orch.   V   PL7090
    (Also contained in)   Vox   VBX1

Violin Concerto in D major, Op. 61
    with Yehudi Menuhin (vln), New Philh.   H   ALP2285/**ASD2285**
                                           A   36369/**S36369**
                                           A   **S–3727C**

Choral Fantasia, Op. 80
    Daniel Barenboim (piano), John Alldis Choir,
    New Philh./*Piano Concertos Nos. 1–5*   H   **SLS941**
                                           A   **S3752D–L**

    (Also issued coupled with Piano Concerto
    No. 2)   H   **ASD2608**

Egmont—Incidental music, Op. 84: Overture; Die
    Trommel gerühret; Freudvoll und leidvoll;
    Clärchens Tod
    with Birgit Nilsson (s), Philh.—
        /*Symphony No. 9—mono version only*   C   33CX1575
                                           A   3577B–L

/*Symphony No. 4*	H	**ASD2563**
/*Symphonies Nos. 1–9 and various Overtures*	H	**SLS788**
Overture and two songs only	C	*SEL1609*

Mass in D major, Op. 123, "Missa Solemnis"
    with Ilona Steingrüber (s), Else Schürhoff (c),
    Erich Majkut (t), Otto Weiner (bs), Vienna
    Academy Choir, Vienna Symphony Orch.   V PL6992/PL11430
    with Elisabeth Søderstrøm (s), Marga Höffgen
    (m–s), Waldemar Kmentt (t), Martti Talvela
    (bs), New Philh. Orch. & Chorus

	H	AN165–6/**SAN165–6**
	H	RLS922/**SLS922**
	A	3679B/**S–3679B**

Fidelio—complete recording
    with Christa Ludwig (m–s), Ingeborg Hallstein
    (s), John Vickers (t), Gerhard Unger (t),
    Walter Berry (br), Gottlob Frick (bs), Franz
    Crass (bs), Philh. Orch & Chorus

	C	33CX1804–6/**SAX2451–3**
		CMS1014/**SMS1014**
Excerpts from complete recording	A	3625C–L/**S–3625C–L**
	A	36168/**S–36168**
	C	33CX1907/**SAX2547**

BERLIOZ
Symphonie fantastique, Op. 14
    Philh.

	C	33CX1898/**SAX2537**
	A	36196/**S–36196**

BRAHMS
Symphonies—
    No. 1 in C minor, Op. 68
    Philh.

	C	33CX1504/**SAX2262**
	A	35481/**S–35481**
	H	**ASD2705**

    No. 2 in D major, Op. 73
    Philh./*Tragic Overture*

	C	33CX1517/**SAX2362**
	A	35532/**S–35532**
	H	**ASD2706**

    No. 3 in F major, Op. 90
    Philh./*Academic Festival Overture*

	C	33CX1536/**SAX2351**
	A	35545/**S–35545**
	H	**ASD2707**

No. 4 in E minor, Op. 98
Philh./

C   33CX1591/**SAX2350**
A   35546/**S–35546**
H   **ASD2708**

Nos. 1–4; Tragic Overture; Academic Festival
Overture
Philh.

H   **SLS804**
A   3614D/**S–3614D**

Academic Festival Overture, Op. 80
Philh./*Symphony No. 3*

C   33CX1536/**SAX2351**
A   35545/**S–35545**
H   **ASD2708**

Tragic Overture, Op. 81
Philh./*Symphony No. 2*

C   33CX1517/**SAX2362**
A   35532/**S–35532**
H   **ASD2706**

/*Brahms: A German Requiem: Alto Rhapsody*   H   **SLS821**
Variations on the St Antoni Chorale, Op. 56
Philh./*Hindemith: Nobilissima Visione*

C   33CX1241
A   35221
A-Sera   60004

Violin Concerto in D major, Op. 77
with David Oistrakh (vln), French National
Radio Orch.

C   33CX1765/**SAX2411**
A   35546/**S–35546**

Alto Rhapsody, Op. 53
with Christa Ludwig (m-s), Philh. Orch. and
Men's Chorus
/*Wagner: Wesendonklieder; Tristan und
Isolde—Liebestod*

C   33CX1817/**SAX2462**
A   35923/**S–35923**

/*Mahler: Des Knaben Wunderhorn—excerpts;
Rückert Lieder—excerpts; Wagner: Wesen-
donklieder*

H   **ASD2391**

/*Brahms: A German Requiem: Tragic Over-
ture*

H   **SLS821**

A German Requiem, Op.45
with Elisabeth Schwarzkopf (s), Dietrich Fischer-
Dieskau (br), Philh. Orch. & Chorus

C   33CXS1781, 33CX1782/
SAX2430, SAX2341
A   3624B–L/**S–3624B–L**

/*Brahms: Alto Rhapsody; Tragic Overture*   H   **SLS821**

BRUCKNER
Symphonies—
    No. 4 in E flat major, "Romantic"
    Vienna Symphony Orch.   V   PL6930/GBY11200
    Philh.   C   33CX1928/**SAX2569**
                                        A   36245/**S36245**

    No. 5 in B flat major
    New Philh.   C   **SAX5288–9**
                                        A   **S–3709B**

    No. 6 in A major
    Philh.   C   33CX1943/**SAX2582**
                                        A   36271/**S36271**

    No. 7 in E major
    Philh./*Wagner: Siegfried Idyll*   C   33CX1808–9/**SAX2454–5**
                                        A   3626B/**S–3626B**

    No. 8 in C minor (Novak edition)
    New Philh. (two cuts in last movement made by
        Dr Klemperer)   H   To be released
    No. 9 in D minor
    New Philh.   H   **ASD2719**

CHOPIN
Piano Concerto No. 2 in F minor, Op. 21
    with Guiomar Novaes (pf), Vienna Symphony
        Orch./*Schumann: Piano Concerto*   V   PL7100/PL11380
DVORAK
Symphony No. 9 in E minor, Op. 95, "From the
    New World"
    Philh.   C   33CX1914/**SAX2554**
                                        A   36246/**S–36246**

FRANCK
Symphony in D minor
    New Philh.   C   CX5276/**SAX5276**
                                        A   36416/**S–36416**

GLUCK
Iphigénie en Aulide—Overture (arr. Wagner)
    Philh./*Weber and Humperdinck Overtures*   C   33CX1770/**SAX2417**
                                        A   36175/**S–36175**

HANDEL
Concerto Grosso in A minor, Op. 6 No. 4
    Philh./*Mozart: Serenade No. 13*   C   33C1053/**SBO2751**
        /*Mozart: Serenade No. 13; Symphony No.*
        25   C   CX5252/**SAX5252**
    also issued as   C   SEL1594/*ESL6254*

Messiah—complete recording
   with Elisabeth Schwarzkopf (s), Grace Hoffman
     (c), Nicolai Gedda (t), Jerome Hines (bs),
     Philh. Orch. & Chorus   H AN146–8/**SAN146–8**
                                  H RLS915/**SLS915**
                                  A 3657C–L/**S–3657C–L**

   Excerpts from complete recording   A 36324/**S–36324**
                                    H ALP2288/**ASD2288**

HAYDN
Symphonies—
   No. 88 in G major
   No. 104 in D major, "London"
   Philh.   C 33CX1931/**SAX2571**
                                    A 36346/**S36346**

   No. 92 in G major, "Oxford"
   No. 95 in C minor
   New Philh.   H **ASD2818**
   No. 98 in B flat major
   No. 101 in D major, "Clock"
   Philh.   C 33CX1748/**SAX2395**
                                    A 35872/**S–35872**

   No. 100 in G major, "Military"
   No. 102 in B flat major
   New Philh.   C CX5266/**SAX5266**
                                    A 36364/**S36364**

HINDEMITH
Nobilissima visione—Ballet Suite
   Philh./*Brahms: St Antoni Variations*   C 33CX1241
                                    A 35221
                             Sera 60004

HUMPERDINCK
Hansel and Gretel—Overture and Dream Pantomime
   Philh./*Gluck and Weber Overtures*   C 33CX1770/**SAX2417**
                                    A 36175/**S–36175**

KLEMPERER
Symphony No. 2
   New Philh./*Klemperer: String Quartet No. 7*
     (Philharmonia Quartet)   H **ASD2572**
Merry Waltz
   Philh./*Johann Strauss II and Weill*   C 33CX1814/**SAX2460**
                                    A 35927/**S–35927**

H

LISZT
Piano Concerto No. 1 in E flat major, S124
    with Annie Fischer (pf), Philh.
       |*Schumann: Piano Concerto*   C 33CX1842/**SAX2485**
MAHLER
Symphonies—
    No. 2 in C minor, "Resurrection"
    Ilona Steingruber (s), Hilde Rössl-Majdan (c),
        Vienna Academy Choir, Vienna Singverein
        Chorus, Vienna Symphony Orch.   V PL7012
          |*Mahler: Das Lied von der Erde*   VBX115
    with Elisabeth Schwarzkopf (s), Hilde Rössl-
        Majdan (c), Philh. Orch & Chorus   C 33CX1829–30/**SAX2473–4**
                                             A 3634B/**S–3634B**
                                           H **SLS806**

    No. 4 in G major
    with Elisabeth Schwarzkopf (s), Philh.   C 33CX1793/**SAX2441**
                                             A 35289/**S–35289**
                                           H **ASD2799**

    No. 7
    New Philh.   H **ASD2491–2, SLS781**
                                           A **S–3740B**

    No. 9
    New Philh.   C SAX5281–2
                                           A **S–3708B**

Des Knaben Wunderhorn—Das irdische Leben; Wo
    die schönen Trompeten blasen
        Christa Ludwig (m–s), Philh./*Rückert Lieder—*
          excerpts;
          |*Brahms: Alto Rhapsody*   H **ASD2391**
Rückert Lieder—Ich atmet' einem linden Duft; Ich bin
    der Welt abhanden gekommen; Um Mitternacht
        Christa Ludwig (m–s), Philh./*Des Knaben*
        Wunderhorn—excerpts;
          |*Brahms: Alto Rhapsody*   H **ASD2391**
          |*Das Lied von der Erde*   A 3704B/**S–3704B**
Das Lied von der Erde
    with Elsa Cavelti (c), Anton Dermota (t), Vienna
        Symphony Orch.   V PL7000/GBY11890
          |*Mahler: Symphony No. 2*   VBX115
    with Christa Ludwig (m–s), Philh. & Fritz
        Wunderlich (t), New Philh.   H AN179/**SAN179**
          |*Mahler songs sung by C. Ludwig*   A 3704B/**S–3704B**

MENDELSSOHN
Symphonies—
    No. 3 in A minor, Op. 56, "Scotch"
    Vienna Symphony Orch.   V PL7080/PL11840
    Philh./*Hebrides Overture*   C 33CX1736/**SAX2342**
                                    A 35880/**S–35880**

    No. 4 in A major, Op. 90, "Italian"
    Vienna Symphony Orch.—
        /*Schubert: Symphony No. 4*   V PL7860/PL11880
        /*Cello Sonata No. 1*   V PL6980
        /*Overtures not conducted by Klemperer* Fidelio ATL4043
    Philh./*Schumann: Symphony No. 4*   C 33CX1751/**SAX2398**
                                      A 35629/**S–35629**

A Midsummer Night's Dream—incidental music
    with Heather Harper (s), Janet Baker (c), Philh.
    Orch. & Chorus   C 33CX1746/**SAX2393**
                                      A 35881/**S–35881**

Hebrides Overture, Op. 26, "Fingal's Cave"
    Philh./*Symphony No. 3*   C 33CX1736/**SAX2342**
                                    A 35880/**S–35880**

MOZART
Symphonies—
    No. 25 in G minor, K183
    Paris Pro Musica Orch./*No. 36*   AmV PL6280
                                          PL11820

    Philh./*No. 40*   C 33CX1457/**SAX2278**
                                      A 35407/**S–35407**

        /*Handel: Concerto Grosso in A minor, Op. 6,*
            No. 4; Mozart: Serenade No. 13   C CX5252/**SAX5252**
    No. 29 in A major, K201
    Philh./*No. 41*   C 33CX1257
                                      A 35209

    New Philh./*No. 33*   C CX5256/SAX5256
                                    A 36329/S–36329

    No. 31 in D major, K297, "Paris"
    Philh./*No. 34*   C 33CX1906/**SAX2546**
                                      A 36216/**S–36216**

    No. 33 in B flat major, K319
    New Philh./*No. 29*   C CX5256/**SAX5256**
                                    A 36329/**S–36329**

    No. 34 in C major, K334
    Philh./*No. 31*   C 33CX1906/**SAX2546**
                                      A 36216/**S–36216**

No. 35 in D major, K385, "Haffner"
Philh./*No. 36; Die Entführung—Overture*   C 33CX1786/**SAX2436**
A 36128/**S-36128**

No. 36 in C major, K425, "Linz"
Paris Pro Musica Orch./*Symphony No. 25*   AmV PL6280/PL11820
Philh./*No. 35; Die Entführung—Overture*   C 33CX1786/**SAX2436**
A 36216/**S-36216**

No. 38 in D major, K504, "Prague"
Philh./*No. 39*   C 33CX1486
A 35408

Philh./*No. 39*   C 33CX1824/**SAX2468**
A 36129/**S-36129**

No. 39 in E flat major, K543
Philh./*No. 38*   C 33CX1486
A 35408

Philh./*No. 38*   C 33CX1824/**SAX2468**
A 36129/**S-36129**

No. 40 in G minor, K550
Philh./*No. 25*   C 33CX1457/**SAX2278**
A 35407/**S-35407**

Philh./*No. 41*   C 33CX1843/**SAX2486**
A 36183/**S-36183**

No. 41 in C major, K551, "Jupiter"
Philh./*No. 29*   C 33CX1257
A 35209

Philh./*No. 40*   C 33CX1843/**SAX2486**
A 36183/**S-36183**

Piano Concerto No. 25 in C major, K503
with Daniel Barenboim (pf), New Philh.
/*Serenade No. 12*   C CX5290/**SAX5290**
A 36536/**S-36536**

Horn Concertos—
No. 1 in D major, K412; No. 2 in E flat major,
K417; No. 3 in E flat major, K 447; No. 4 in
E flat major, K495
with Alan Civil (horn), Philh./   C 33CX1760/**SAX2406**
A 35689/**S-35689**

Adagio and Fugue in C minor, K546
Philh./*Mozart: Serenade No. 6; Beethoven: Grosse
Fuge*   C 33CX1438
A 35401
C 33CX1948/**SAX2587**
A 36289/**S-36289**

Masonic Funeral Music, K477
New Philh./*Overtures; Adagio and Fugue*   C 33CX1948/**SAX2587**
                  A 36289/**S–36289**

Overtures—
 Le Nozze di Figaro, K492(b); Die Entführung
 aus dem Serail, K384(a)§; Don Giovanni,
 K527(b) (with concert ending by Dr
 Klemperer); Così fan tutte, K588(b); La
 Clemenza di Tito, K621(b); Die Zauberflöte,
 K620(a)
 Philh. (a) and New Philh. (b)/*Masonic Funeral*
 Music; Adagio and Fugue   C 33CX1948/**SAX2587**
                  A 36289/**S–36289**

 Item marked § also issued   C 33CX1786/**SAX2436**
                  A 36128/**S–36128**

Serenades
 No. 6 in D major, K239, "Serenata Notturna"
 Philh./*Mozart: Adagio and Fugue; Beethoven:*
 Grosse Fuge   C 33CX1438
                  A 35401

 No. 10 in B flat major, K361
 London Wind Quintet & Ensemble   C CX5259/**SAX5259**
                  A 36247/**S–36247**

 No. 11 in E flat major, K375
 New Philh. Wind Ensemble   H To be released
 No. 12 in C minor, K388
 New Philh. Wind Ensemble/*Piano Concerto No.*
 25   C CX5290/**SAX5290**
                  A 36536/**S36536**

 No. 13 in G major, K525, "Eine kleine Nacht-
 musik"
 Paris Pro Musica Orch. (*c.* 1947) AmV 169★
               AmV VLP1690

 Philh./*Handel: Concerto Grosso in A minor, Op. 6*
 No. 4   C 33C1053/**SBO2751**
 New Philh./*Handel: Concerto Grosso in A minor,*
 Op. 6 No. 6; Mozart: Symphony No. 25 C CX5252/**SAX5252**
COSÌ FAN TUTTE, K588—complete recording
 with Margaret Price (s), Yvonne Minton (m-s),
 Lucia Popp (s), Luigi Alva (t), Sir Geraint
 Evans (br), Hans Sotin (bs), New Philh.,
 John Alldis Choir   H **SLS961**

DON GIOVANNI, K527—complete recording
    with Nicolai Ghiaurov (bs), Walter Berry (br),
    Nicolia Gedda (t), Franz Crass (bs), Mirella
    Freni (s), Christa Ludwig (m-s), Claire
    Watson (s), New Philh. Orch. & Chorus

H	AN172–5/**SAN172–5**
H	RLS923/**SLS923**
A	3700D–L/**S–3700D–L**

    Excerpts from complete recording   H **ASD2508**

LE NOZZE DI FIGARO, K492—complete recording
    with Sir Geraint Evans (br), Teresa Berganza
    (m-s), Elisabeth Søderstrøm (s), Gabriel
    Bacquier (br), Reri Grist (s), Annelies Bur-
    meister (c), Michael Langdon (bs), John Alldis
    Choir, New Philh.   H **SLS955**

DIE ZAUBERFLÖTE, K620—complete recording
    with Gundula Janowitz (s), Nicolai Gedda (t),
    Walter Berry (br), Ruth-Margaret Pütz (s),
    Gottlob Frick (bs), Franz Crass (bs), Lucia
    Popp (s), Philh. Orch. & Choir

H	AN137–9/**SAN137–9**
H	RLS912/**SLS912**
A	3651C–L/**S–3651CL**

    Excerpts from complete recording

H	ALP2314/**ASD2314**
A	36315/**S–36315**

RAMEAU
Gavotte with Six Variations (orchestrated Klemperer)
New Philh./*Beethoven: Symphony No. 7*   H **ASD2537**

SCHUBERT
Symphonies—
    No. 4 in C minor, D 417, "Tragic"
    Lamoureux Orch.

/Symphony No. 5 not conducted by Klemperer	V	GBY11880
/Mendelssohn: Symphony No. 4	V	PL11880
/Schubert: Arpeggione Sonata	V	PL6800

No. 5 in B flat major, D485
Philh./*Symphony No. 8*

C	33CX18670/**SAX2514**
A	36164/**S–36164**

No. 8 in B minor, D759, "Unfinished"
Philh./*Symphony No. 5*

C	33CX1870/**SAX2514**
A	36164/**S–36164**

No. 9 in C major, D944, "Great"
Philh.

C	33CX1754/**SAX2397**
A	35946/**S–35946**

SCHUMANN
Symphonies—
    No. 1 in B flat major, Op. 38, "Spring"
    New Philh./*Manfred Overture*

C CX5269/**SAX5269**
A 36353/**S–36353**

    No. 2 in C major, Op. 61
    New Philh./*Genoveva—Overture*

H **ASD2454**
A **S–36606**

    No. 3 in E flat major, Op. 97, "Rhenish"
    New Philh./*Faust—Overture*

H **ASD2547**
A **S–36689**

    No. 4 in D minor, Op. 120
    Philh./*Mendelssohn: Symphony No. 4*

C 33CX1751/**SAX2398**
A 35927/**S–35927**

    Genoveva—Overture, Op. 81
    New Philh./*Symphony No. 2*

H **ASD2454**
A **S–36606**

    Faust—Overture
    New Philh./*Symphony No. 3*

H **ASD2547**
A **S–36689**

    Manfred—Overture, Op. 115
    New Philh./*Symphony No. 1*

C 33CX5269/**SAX5269**
A 36353/**S–36353**

Piano Concerto in A minor, Op. 54
    Guiomar Novaes (pf), Vienna Symphony Orch.
        /*Chopin: Piano Concerto No. 2*

V PL7110/PL11380

    Annie Fischer (pf), Philh.
        /*Liszt: Piano Concerto No. 1*

C 33CX1842/**SAX2485**

JOHANN STRAUSS II
Weiner Blut—Waltz, Op. 354
Kaiser Waltz—Op. 437
Die Fledermaus—Overture
    Philh./*Klemperer and Weill*

C 33CX1814/**SAX2460**
A 35972/**S–35972**

RICHARD STRAUSS
Don Juan, Op. 20
Till Eulenspiegel, Op. 28
Salome—Dance of the Seven Veils
    Philh.

C 33CX1715/**SAX2367**
A 35737/**S–35737**

Tod und Verklärung, Op. 24
Metamorphosen
    Philh.

C 33CX1789/**SAX2437**

STRAVINSKY
Pulcinella—Suite
    Philh./*Symphony in Three Movements*   C 33CX1949/**SAX2588**
                                    A Sera **S–60188**

Symphony in Three Movements
    Philh./*Pulcinella—Suite*   C 33CX1949/**SAX2588**
                                      A Sera **S–60188**

TCHAIKOVSKY
Symphonies—
    No. 4 in F minor, Op. 36
    Philh.   C 33CX1852/**SAX2494**
                                      A 36134/**S–36134**

    No. 5 in E minor, Op. 64
    Philh.   C 33CX1854/**SAX2497**
                                      A 36141/**S–36141**

    No. 6 in B minor, Op. 74, "Pathétique"
    Philh.   C 33CX1812/**SAX2458**
                                      A 35787/**S–35787**

    Nos. 4–6 as a three-record boxed set   A 3711C/**S–3711C**

WAGNER
Siegfried Idyll (original scoring)
    Philh./*Bruckner: Symphony No. 7*   C 33CX1809/**SAX2455**
                                      A 3626B/**S–3626B**

DER FLIEGENDE HOLLÄNDER—complete recording
    with Theo Adam (br), Martti Talvela (bs), Anja
        Silja (s), Annelies Burmeister (c), Ernst Kozub
        (t), Gerhard Unger (t), BBC Chorus, New
        Philh.   H **SAN207–9, SLS934**
                                      A **S3730C–L**

    Excerpts from complete recording   H **ASD2724**
TRISTAN UND ISOLDE—Liebestod
    with Christa Ludwig (m–s), Philh.
        /*Wagner: Wesendonklieder;*
        /*Brahms: Alto Rhapsody*   C 33CX1817/**SAX2462**
DIE WALKÜRE—Act I (complete)
    with Helga Dernesch (s), William Cochran (t),
        Hans Sotin (bs), New Philh.   H /**SLS968**
DIE WALKÜRE—Leb' Wohl; Magic Fire Music
    with Norman Bailey (bass-br), New Philh. H /**SLS968**
"Klemperer conducts Wagner"
    Rienzi—Overture
    Der Fliegende Holländer—Overture

Tannhäuser—Overture
‡Lohengrin—Prelude to Act 1
  Philh.

    C 33CX1697/**SAX2347**
    A 3610B/**S–3610B**
    A 36187/**S–36187**
    H **ASD2695**

Lohengrin—Prelude to Act 3
Die Meistersinger von Nürnberg—Prelude to
  Act I; †Dance of the Apprentices; †Procession
  of the Masters
Tristan und Isolde—Prelude and Liebestod
†Götterdämmerung—Funeral Music
  Philh.

    C 33CX1698/**SAX2348**
    A 3610B/**S–3610B**
    A 36188/**S–36188**
    H **ASD2696**

"Klemperer conducts more Wagner"
  Das Rheingold—Entry of the Gods
  ‡Die Walküre—Ride of the Valkyries
  Siegfried—Forest Murmurs
  Götterdämmerung—Siegfried's Rhine Journey
  Tannhäuser—Prelude to Act 3
  Parsifal: Prelude
  Philh.

    C 33CX1820/**SAX2464**
    A 35947/**S–35947**
    H **ASD2697**

    Items marked ‡ also issued on
    Items marked † also issued on

    C *SEL1677*/**ESL6283**
    C *scd2178*

Wesendonklieder
  with Christa Ludwig (m-s), Philh.
    /Brahms: Alto Rhapsody; Wagner: Tristan
    und Isolde—Liebestod

    C 33CX1817/**SAX2462**
    A 35923/**S–35923**

    /Brahms: Alto Rhapsody; Mahler: Des
    Knaben Wunderhorn—excerpts; Rückert
    Lieder—excerpts

    H **ASD2391**

WEBER
Der Freischütz—Overture
Euryanthe—Overture
Oberon—Overture
  Philh./*Gluck and Humperdinck*

    C 33CX1770/**SAX2417**
    A 36175/**S–36175**

WEILL
Kleine Dreigroschenmusik
    Philh./*Johann Strauss and Klemperer*   C 33CX1814/**SAX2460**
                                        A 35927/**S–35927**

The compiler wishes to express his thanks to Link House Publications Ltd., the publishers of *Hi-Fi News & Record Review* and Miss Lotte Klemperer for assistance in the preparation of this discography.

MALCOLM WALKER
February 1973

Index

Details after personal entries relate only to the context in which they are discussed in the text.